GOD

Guiding Poetry to a
Higher Consciousness

© 2023 Rumi Bumi
All rights reserved

God.

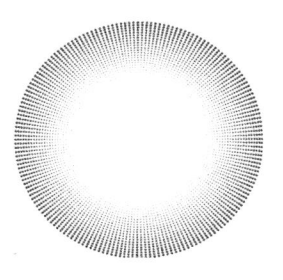

Chapter 1: Reality/ space

The Beauty of All Things
In every single thing,
all is one.

Made exactly the same.

Everything ever saw.

Equivalent;

No difference at all.

Not this,
not that.

No you,
nor me.

Made in the extraordinary beauty of all things.

As Above, So Below
Everything, sun,
everything sand.

Manifested hydrogen.

As above, so below.

The stars in the sky
are the ground beneath our feet.

Compacted into a breathing seed.

The existence of skin, stone and bone inside every sun ever shone.

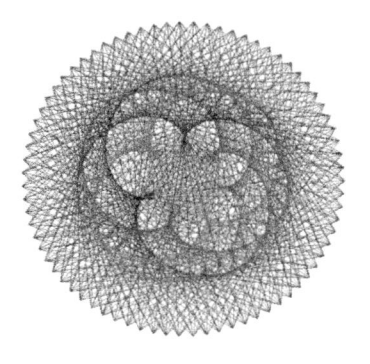

Fundamental Existence
Fundamentals of existence:

Chemical reaction.

Motion, mind.

Awareness.

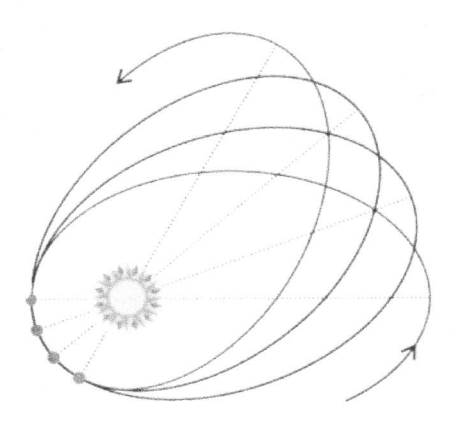

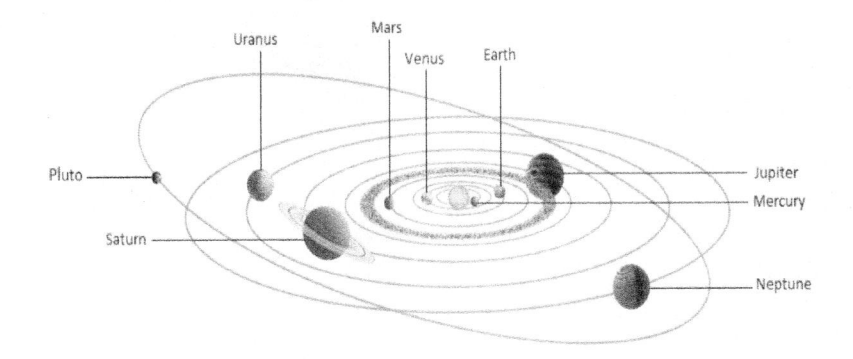

Microscope/ telescope
Under a microscope,
I see the sun.

Mars in rust.

Venus, a speck of dust.

So Jupiter and Saturn.

Solar system and universe.

Gaze upward.

Eye be your microscope.

See furthest out, look down.

Eyes be your telescope.

Fractal Universe
No edge and no center.

The universe goes on forever.

From dust, to planet.

Endless.

Infinitely finite
fractal universe.

Space
Stars, planets and moons.

All that exists.

No matter what it is.

Space.

What you see, hear, smell, touch and taste.

Experiences before you.

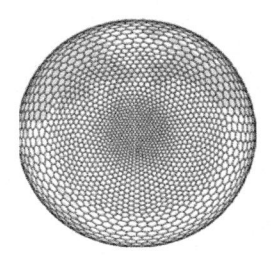

Without Beginning/ without end
It is difficult to comprehend;

No beginning and no end.

But nothing comes in
or vanishes from existence.

Universally recycled to come back again.

Something has always been.

One/ one reality/ the universe
By the atom, we are attached.

One inside another.

You,
me,

Out there, right here.

As *one reality*
we call

the universe.

"Motion"/ "vibration"
Knowledge of motion are the missing key.

I see a very soon solution coming.

You will be the one to speak.

The answers of reality.

Radiation. Magnetism.

All there can ever be.

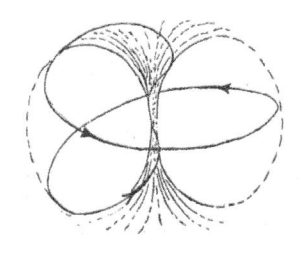

Acceleration/ the non existing zero space
The universe falls into itself.

Constant motion,
trading places
to fill the infinite lesser place.

Accelerating toward the non existent zero space.

Precession/ spin/ to never touch zero
Round and round, without rest.

Wobbles and flips.

As a wooden spoon, stirs soup in the pot.

So stars stirred in the galaxy.

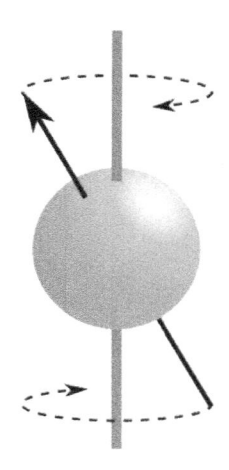

"Matter"/ "atom"/ "black hole"
Space.

The eye of god.

Dancing and burning.

Colours
swirling.

One inside another
that makes up
the Universe.

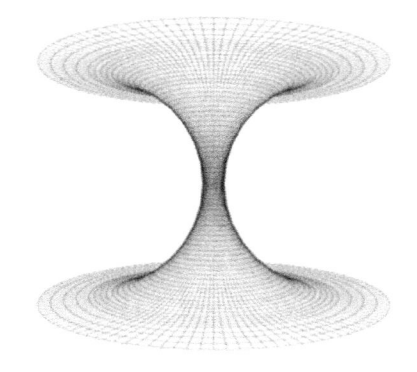

"Galactic Jet"
Simultaneously inducting and radiating.

Space flows in perfect symmetry.

Inhale, breathe.

The universe,
illuminating.

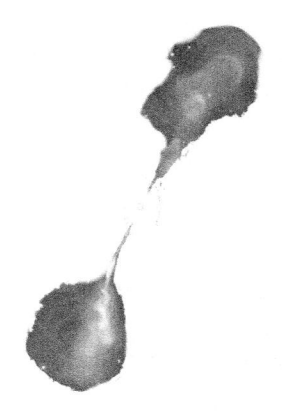

Spiral/ the intelligence of nature/ the memory of nature
Remaining balanced in the lowest pressure.

Effortlessly in the middle.

Natures intelligence;

Efficient.

Working less to get more.

Compression.

Discharging.

Spreading.

Catching water and warmth.

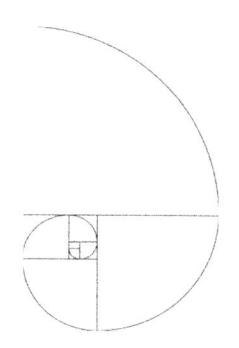

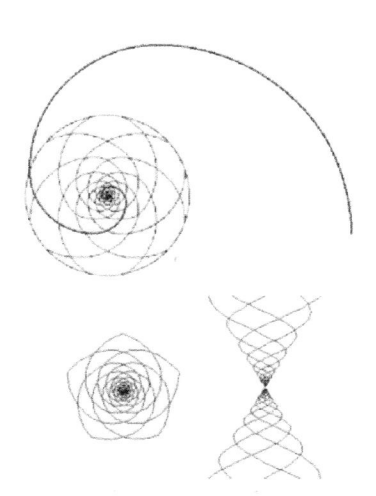

"Vortex" / "poles" / "galaxy"
All that make up physicality;

Minerals of the universe
in flow.

Drain spiraling downward,
upward, simultaneously.

A vortex of matter
pun inside one another other.

Black holes in black holes.

Swirling,
in a poles pole.

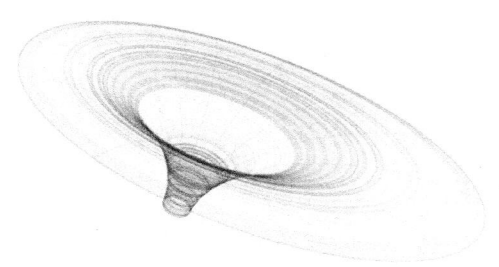

Helix
Heating, cooling in balance
around the center.

Condensed.

Hydrogen to metal.

Water to air,
air to earth,
earth to fire.

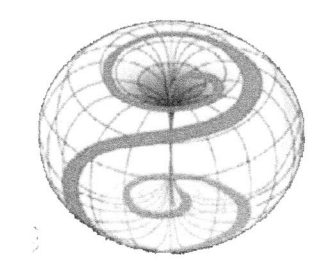

Torus/ toroidal field
Geometry of the universe.

Hypotrochoidal.

Crisscrossing compression.

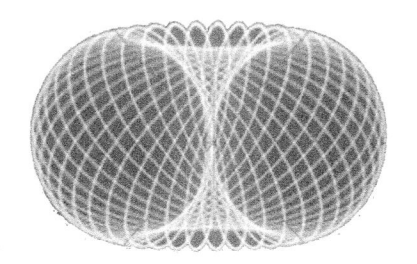

Ether/ secret of space
All history, all existence.

All that has ever been.

Pure potential.

I leave you with the Ether.

Secret of the universe.

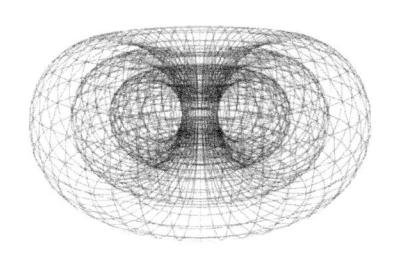

Condensed Space
Hydrogen falling down upon itself.

Self enclosing.

Condensed,
heated into water, rock and metal,
stretched like a balloon.

Hollowing out its center.

Outer Space/ hydrogen field/ the inverse of a magnet
The universe is a magnet.

Every single thing,
magnetic.

Inside,
all.

Outerspace.

Hydrogen.

Space and illumination
in the inverse of a magnet.

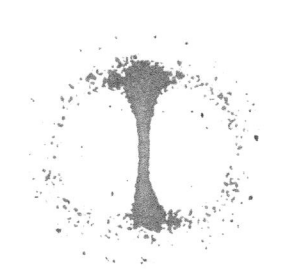

Magnet
Metals,
ideal to view natural mechanics.

Technology.

The universes magic trick.

Null Point/ induction/ chasing the non existing zero
Between the bodies
acceleration toward the lesser space.

The lowest point of energy must be filled.

In a self contained universe,
thrusting, fighting for its place
to violently burn.

Grinding,
heating.

Illuminating.

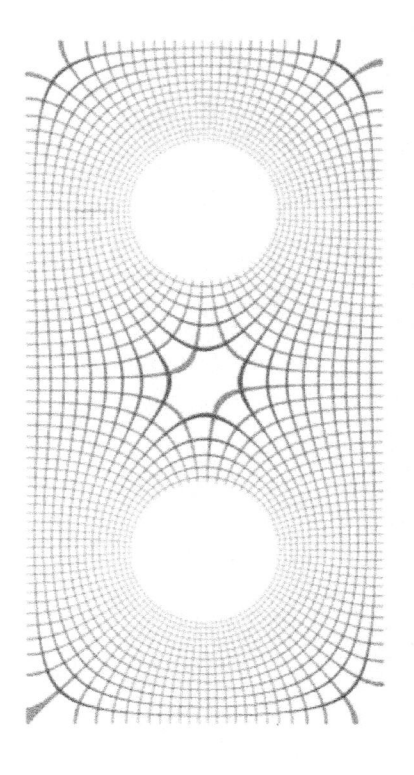

Radiation/ heat
Burning, burning

matter/ mass/ space

Cosmic substance.

Heat.

Back and forth chemical reaction.

Radiation and induction.

"Energy"/ "frequency"/ "vibration"
Motion rules the universe.

All you do and don't see
is the infinity of
everything.

The divinity
of existing.

Potential; Everything
Everything there is
contained in every star, atom and seed.

Every burning core
packed infinitely.

Life,

Potential.

Everything.

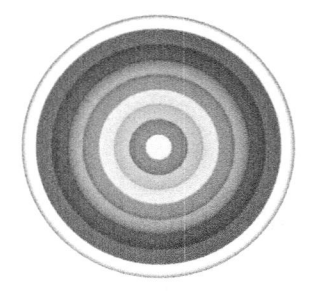

Rainbow universe/ colour
In the density of space,
colour manifests.

Planets, solar system, and universe.

Rainbows.

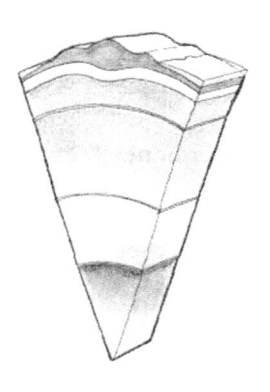

Layers
Layered by elements.

Metal, rock, water, life, air.

Inner core, outer core
mantle, upper mantle.

Crust, plants, ocean.

Atmosphere.

Red, orange, yellow.
Green, blue, indigo.
Violet.

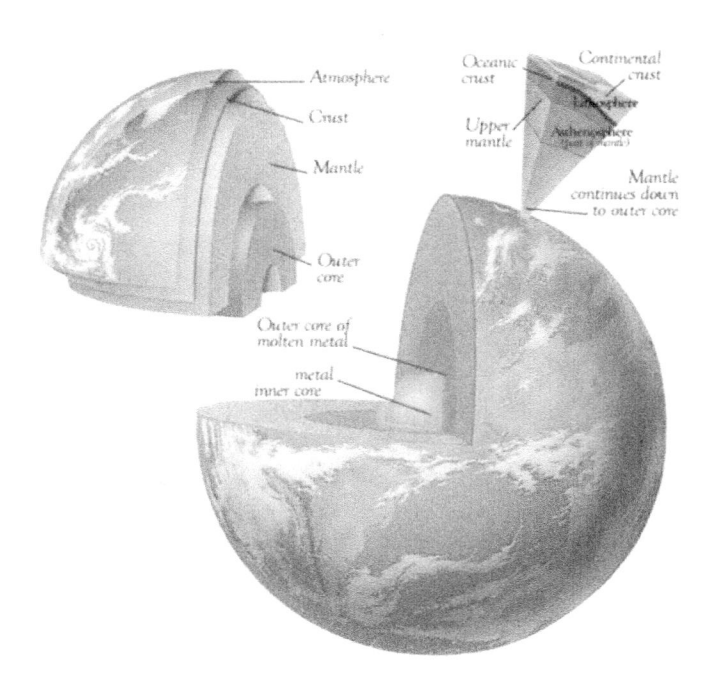

Universal Medium/ permeability
Sand and boulder.

Ocean and rain.

Trade places.

A universal pressure
mediation.

From earth to air,
air to earth.

Iron and hydrogen by water
and fire.

Swapping places.

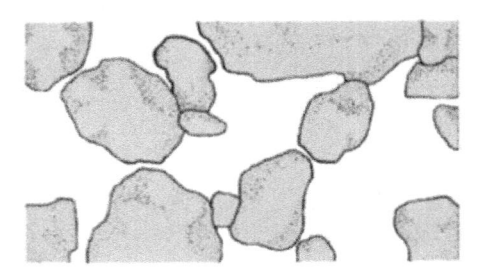

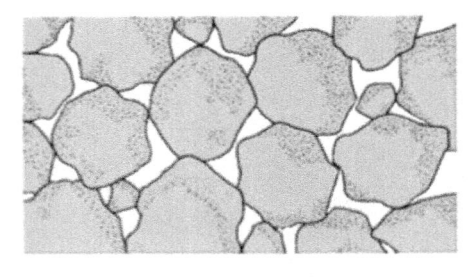

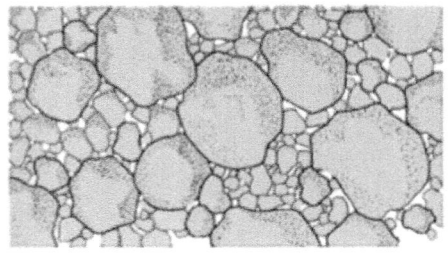

Density/ permittivity
No, you are not quickly bursting into flame,
in pain, are you?

Your body,
layered chemically.

In every form,
all elements;

At different frequency,
atomic densities.

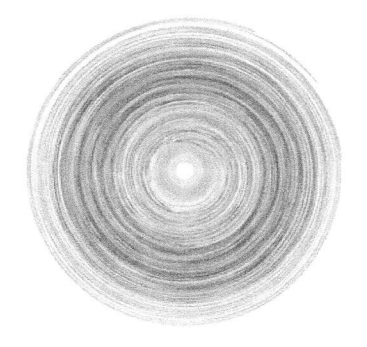

Element
Jewel of the universe.

The beauty of mind.

All that makes the universe breathe.

The Infinite Earth
I am born,
out from the fire,
out from the oceans,
the sky,
the infinite.

Earth.

Physicality/ all things/ in motion

Air is the all.

Earth is the all.

Water is the all.

Fire is the all.

Space is the all

A physical existence in motion.

Infinity.

One.

Inside All Things
Space inside space.

Here, we stand in, and
as all things.

Observant.

Function of the universe.

Fire/ space in motion

In your purest identity,
you are fire.

Space in motion.

The sun,
stars,

lightening,
electricity.

Vibration.

A vein of energy.

Minerals of infinite galaxies.

Water, heat.

Formation,

Burning, cooling, eternally.

Quickly

or slowly.

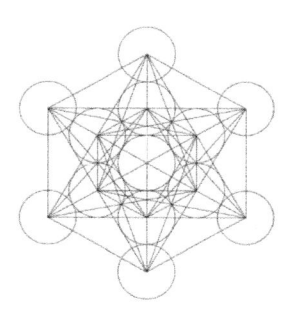

Water
Our role in the universe.

Slowly, dehydrating;

No more do I see liquid in my cup
brought from the ground and sky.

But the universal eye.

Self contained drop.

Inside,
outside itself.

Air/ hydrogen
No thing;

Everything.

Hydrogen manifests into
a denser state of being.

Every color of space.

Earths
from red, to violet.

Water to flame.

Minerals and metals.

Everything is Everything/ impressions
Intense compression.

Air turns to water.

Water turns to earth.

earth to fire.

And fire, to air.

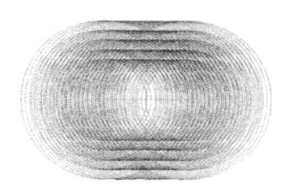

The Split Infinite
By the mighty universe.

The all is infinite.

All one;

Split.

No matter how many times,
elements are incommensurate.

Magnets of the universe.

Potential Space
In the center of everything, is another.

Then, the universe.

Then, the universe.

Deeper deeper, no matter how far you go.

Hollow
The inside of every atom, hollow.

So the sun, and the moon and earth.

Space inside space.

Penetrate into the hollow place.

The eye of the universe.

Iron Dome/ inside a star/ magnetic universe/ core
Gaze up,
at the iron dome.

What man has called stars
since the beginning
is one.

Stars inside a star.

As all things are;

Connected.
Magnetic.

All substance,
chemical, atom, elements.

In a prison of precious
boiling metal.

Stone and Metal/ mineral/magnet/ comet/ asteroid
Dense, compressed potential.

Manifested into stone and metal.

Fusing.
Forming.

Penetrate a layer of water;

Freeze.

Slung around the sun;

Burn.

Molten cooling comets.

Ring around the planets
and stars.

Pushed out from the fire.

Illumination
Day and night.

Behind matter, a shadow.

Facing the star,
burning,
glowing.

Shining through space.

Illuminating the air.

Penetrate the shadow/ giants
Dig upward.

Beyond heaven.

Passed the stars,
enter the firmament.

Penetrate the shadow;

Into the rocky mantle
and metals.

Drill through universal crust.

A new earth.

Giants.

Whole Universe/ balanced atom
Packed tight;

Metals,
rock, plants.

Water, earth, air and fire.

Rising and falling
in rotation with shadow and sun.

Suitable for life.

Balanced temperature.

Tucked away in pockets of perfection.

The whole universe.

A rainbow
in this compacted space.

A view of existence.

Earthling
The all.

The perfect universe.

All that is physical.

The atom.

Nature.

Sound/ disturbance; vibration
An eternal roar.

In fire, clouds,
ocean waves.

A vibration.

Sound.

A disturbance in the medium.

Suns, stars and planets, beating
heating, illuminating.

Discharge/ veins
Sparks.
Static.

Sun.
Fire.

Branches and limbs.

Rivers,
lightening.

Veins of the universe.

Volcano/ a vein of potential
Potential of earths core, tunnels a vein.

Lava;

Heart of the all.

The surface is reached.

Crust ruptured.

Sprouting upward,
a rocky structure.

Smoke and ash filled the air.

Clouds and water accumulated there.

Layer upon layer.

Oxygen, carbon,
soot and soil,
life rose from the dirt.

Conscious beings of the universe.

Placing Seed
Be conscious of life.

Everywhere,
rooted deep.

In every vein of existence.

Reaching arms out to give.

Placing seed.

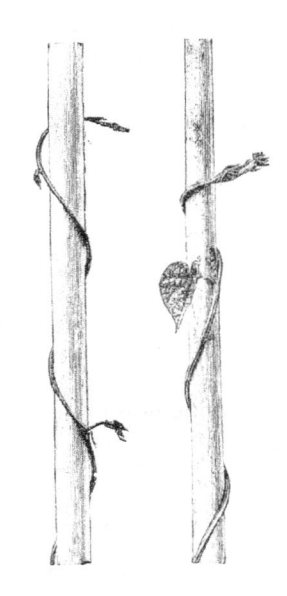

Plane of Life/ the green plane of the universe
Behavior in nature acts,
replicates, the universe.

Mother nature.

Life,
sun.

Planets,
plants,
and animals, fungi
Lie only on the green plane of
the universe

Sprout
Pockets of life sprout from the layers, a seed,
embedded deep.

A tight packed
sprouting being.

Cooked carbon in the mantle.

Metals,
minerals.

Watered, pressure,
expanding.
Breaking the shell.

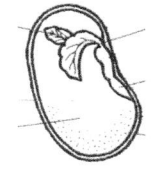

Food/ stem
That which replicates the universe,
good for the body.

Health is of absolute importance.

Ingestion,

separated and distributed
to organs.

Waste, fertilizing nature.

And food delivered back to the universe.

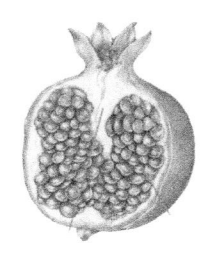

The All/ DNA

Substance of molted feathers,
fur, scales and shell.

Cells, shedding hair and
spilled blood.

Festering carcass.

Dirt of the universe.

Plants and pollen.

Walking upon dust fallen.

Standing up
and out of its skin again.

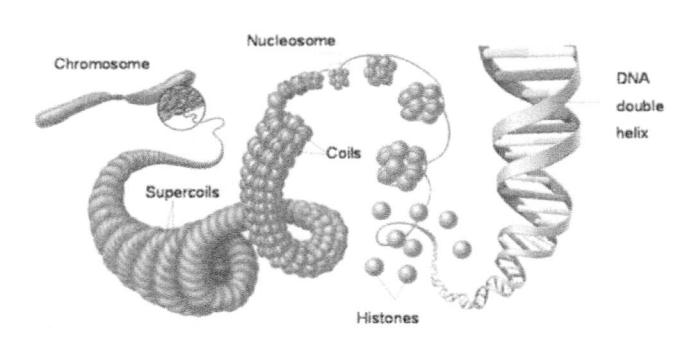

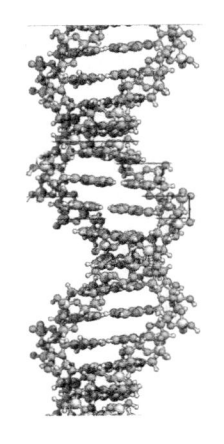

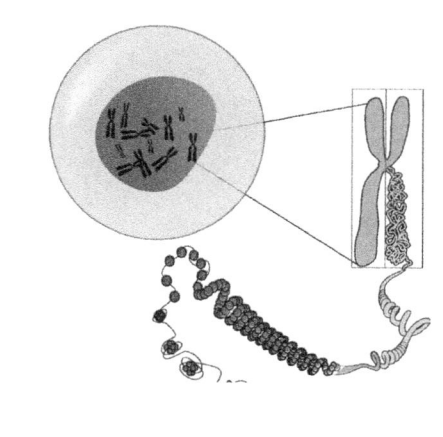

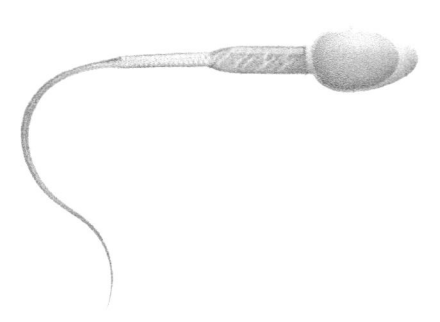

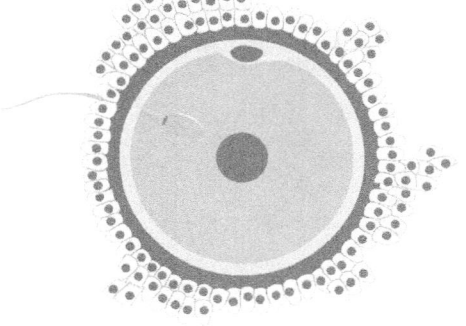

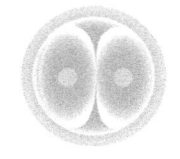

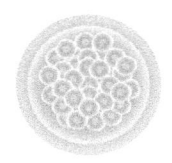

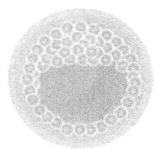

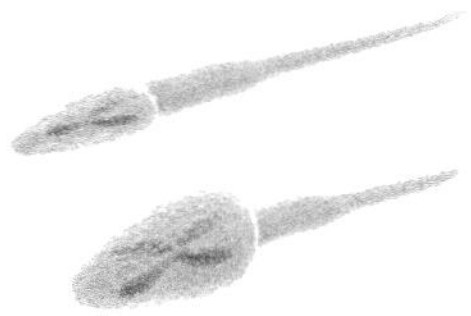

ZYGOTE　　　2 CELL STAGE　　　4 CELL STAGE

8 CELL STAGE　　　MORULA　　　BLASTOCYST

Organism/ cell
I see myself in the animals.

In shape, and behavior;

Intentions

Species running, hissing, chasing.

Imitating.

Under any cost, mating.

Urging to plant its seed;

Multiplying.

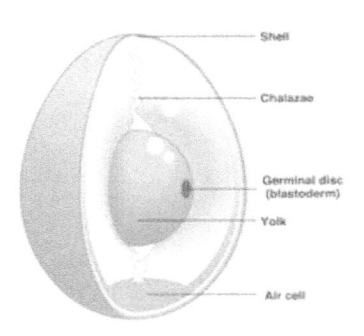

"Egg"/ pocket of life
At perfect temperature,
the egg hatches.

One day, grow to know itself
on the grand miracle of nature.

Potential pocket of life.

Packed away
for a rebirth.

Blood of the All/ elemental memory
Elemental memory.

Minerals are the body.

Down to the iron in your blood.

Traces of the infinite runs through your veins.

And with a pulse, blood is distributed throughout;

Cooled, into tissue.

Pump/ heart/ closed circuit
The bell that rings inside you, sloshes in rhythm of the universe.

Pacing, pumping.

I am the infinite machine.

Perpetually pulsing.

Vibrating

Beating.

I am technology.

Innately shocking.

A closed circuit;

Circulating being.

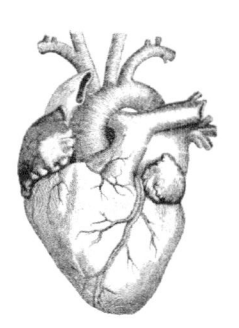

Brain/ neural network
Web of vibration.

Network.

The universe, a nervous system.

A brain.

Inducting,
distributing chemistry.

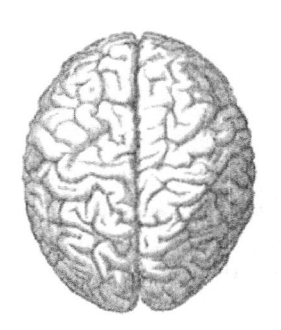

Receiver/ transmitter
Mind,
the Universe,
all;

Sound
taste
smell
touch
and sight.

Nose, ears, mouth, eyes and skin.
Soaking in the universal disturbances.

Information receiving.

Transmitting.

Into,
and from the holes of your being.

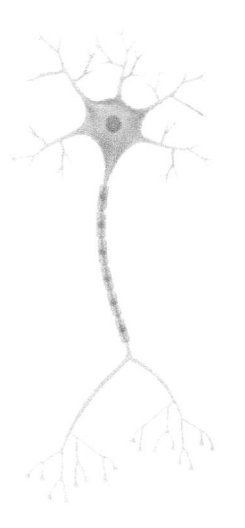

Fire
I've watched the universe
burn.

Again and again.

I can never take my eyes off it.

Artists of the Galaxies
Maps, drawings, inventions.

Blueprints for our taking and evolving.

Secrets and hints,
left by the artists of the galaxies.

Magnets, electricity,

motion.

Patterns of existence.

Decipher messages
as human intelligence is measured.

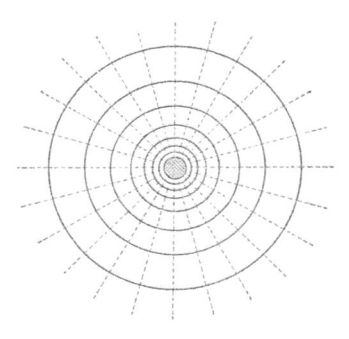

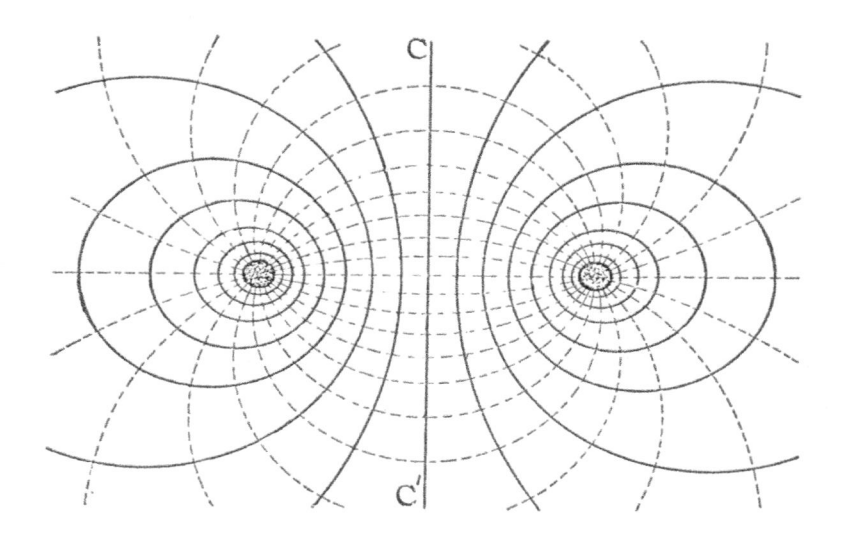

Sacred Geometry/ inevitable art
Left behind,
for an eternity is the art of existence.

Matter, motion;

Mind.

The existing universe.

Vibration.

Secrets of consciousness.

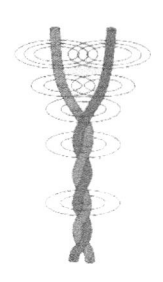

The Inventor

Inventor,
creator;

The answer is within.

Nature works absolutely in torus.

Truth in the fabric.

The inventor asks
"What is existence?"

With an organized mind,
the invention builds itself;

Dismantling the universe.

Down to the fundamental.

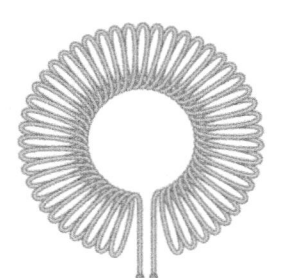

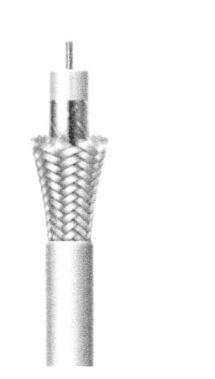

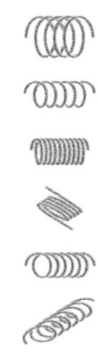

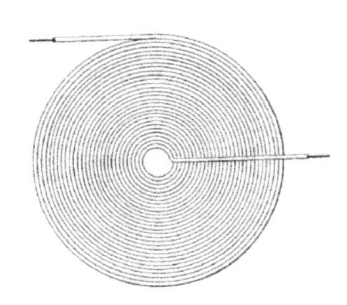

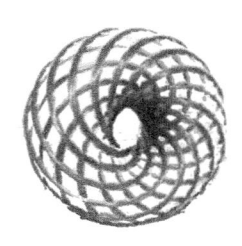

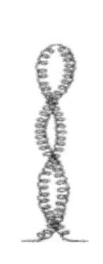

Imitating Atom
Copy nature.

Imitate
the atom in technology.

Metals within metals,
rotating helix.

Coils within coils in the shape of reality by:

Capacitance.
Resistance.
Permeability.

In a torus.

DNA

Radiation by pressure mediation.

Replicating the stars, matter,
black holes;

The Universe.

Eye of Atom/ creating the sun/ manifesting energy
Radiation.

Levitation.

Spin.

Hollow.
Vibrating.
Glowing.

Illuminating.

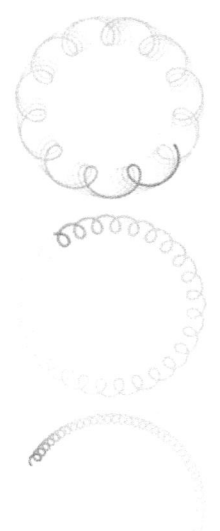

Cycle of Nature/ life is all there is
The seed goes on.

Protected by folds and layer.

Life is all there is.

Stars and planets
become aware of its own cycle of nature.

Chapter 2: Heaven/ nature

Induction and Capacitance/ acceleration/ magnetism

What is absorbed,

induction of radiation.

Capacitance,
acceleration.

Physics of the galaxy.

Sacred geometry.

Discharge and Resistance
Discharge radiation.

Transferring heat.

Held up in resistance.

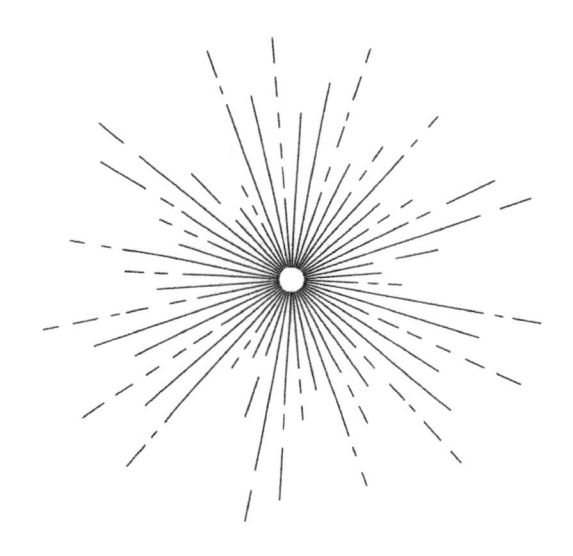

Perception of the Phenomenon
There is nothing,
but the rise and fall of matter.

And perception of the phenomenon.

All else,
an illusion.

The Base Existence/ for mind to interpret
Water
Earth
Fire
Air

Space.

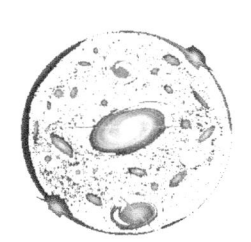

Without name.

The base of existence.

And for the mind to interpret.

Sky
Sky.

Specks of metals, and dusts.

All one.

That
which flows in and out of our lungs.

In which we become,

everything.

Clouds and Lightening
Rising and falling through the earth
and universe.

Condensing,
accumulating of the all.

Clashing in static and compression.

Firing at itself,
a powerful magnet.

Frequency of Self
All you see,
and all you don't
are the delicate,
extreme frequencies
of the mighty being.

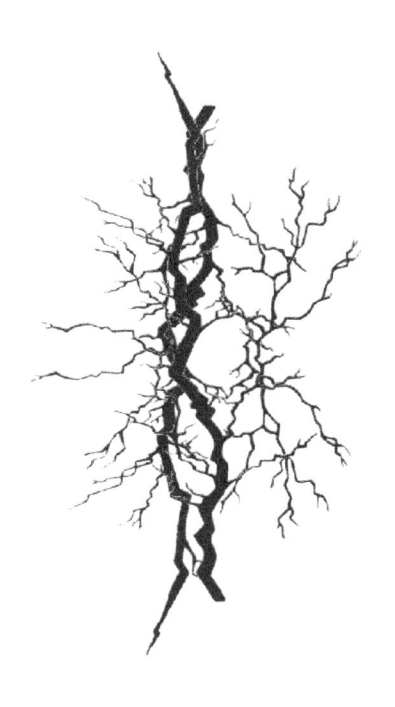

The Art of Reality/ universal pattern
Develop the eye to see.

Master the art of reality.

Find the universal pattern
in everything.

The double helix.

Heat/ radiation
In the warmest,
coolest things.

Radiating frequency.
In the shape of the all.

Cold/ Ice/ lesser heat/ snow/ speck of the all
Temperature comes and goes.

Ice or snow.
Lesser heat.

Fractal frequency.

A speck of the all.

Star/ sun/ core/ molten lava
Look,
deep into the galaxy.

Deeper
into the core of earth.

Find a star.

Sun in the sun.

Surrounding one another.

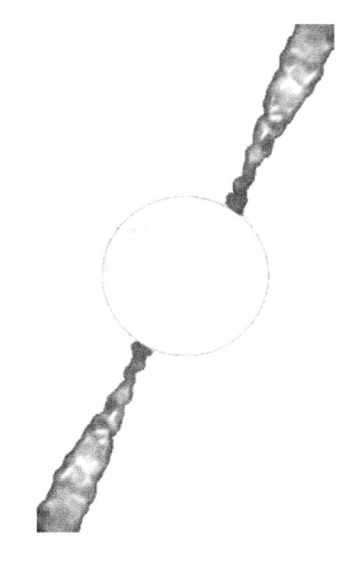

Seeds of Infinity/ ocean of iron/ accumulation of hydrogen
Seeds of infinity
move like water.

An ocean of iron.

The eternal,
infinite cosmos,

compressing
stars within stars.

Welding metals

in the spiraling
flow of motion.

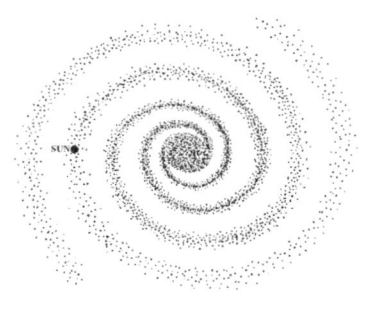

Oxidizing Iron/ rusted earth/ iron and ice/ corrosion
On this ball of everything,
we call Earth;

Iron.
Ice

Rust.

Potential stored away
and released.

Chemical reaction
pushing outward
all frequencies of being.

crust
volcano
ash
carbon
plant

Volcanic Eruption/ smoke/ soot/ rain/ self sufficient
Spouting seed of the inner all.

Molten lava
makes it way
through a tunnel.

Soot is laid,
layered.

And smoke gathers water,
raining upon the planet;

Nurturing all released from the vein.

And the world,
self sufficient.

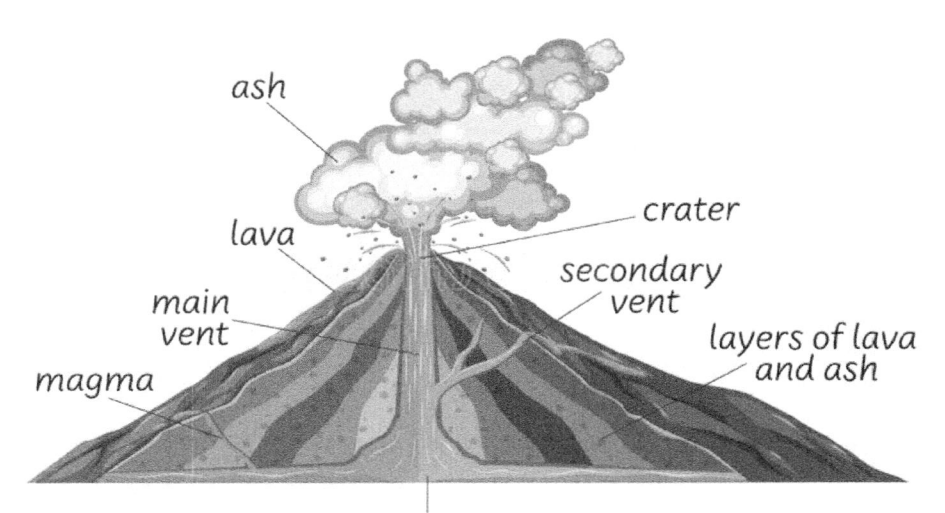

Dirt/soil/ germination
Every blade of grass,
standing tree
and flower;

Mixed into the soil.

Compost,
recycling in the crust.

Balanced upright.

Capacitance, radiation,
breaking through shell
in an up,
down spiral.

South of the seed,
stumped by dirt.

And the north
extended in fractals,
as air is less resistant.

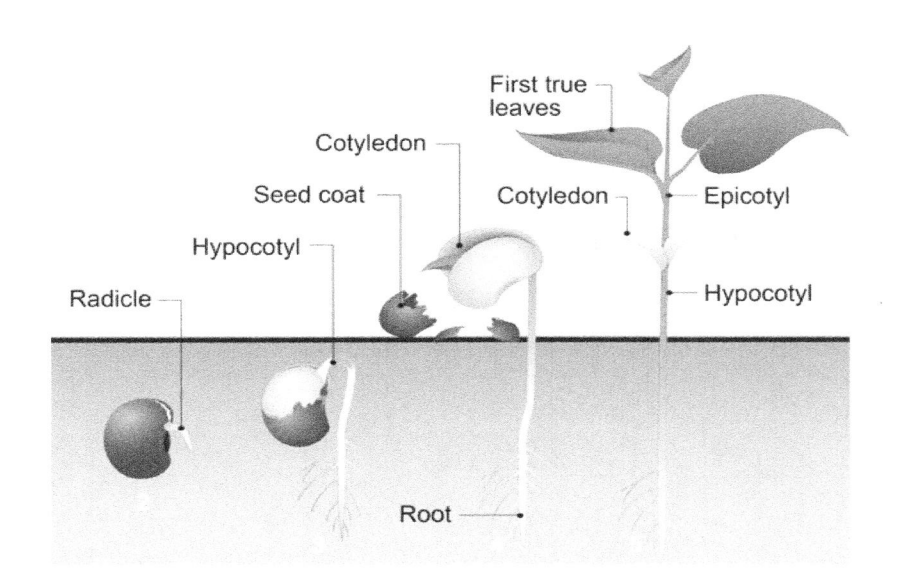

Stem/ vein/ shoots and roots

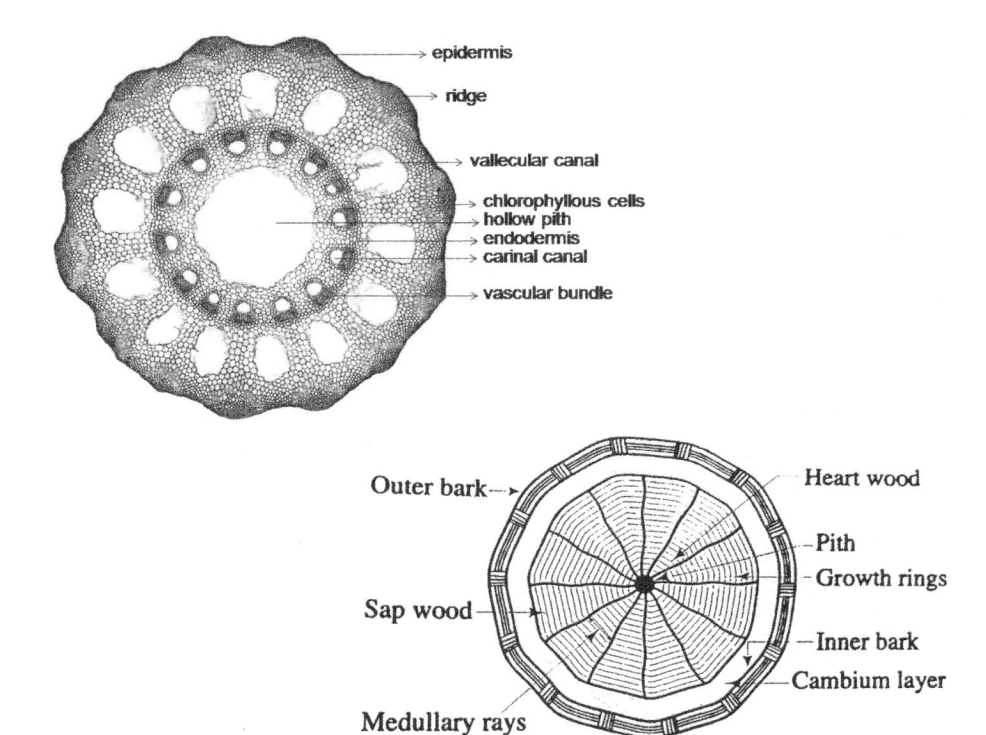

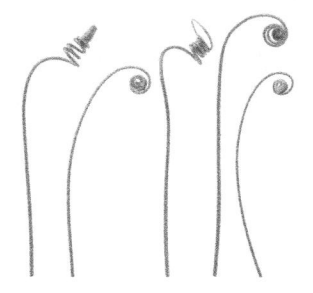

Trees/ slow discharge
Picture me
as static;

Unfolding.

Trees,
very slow lightening.

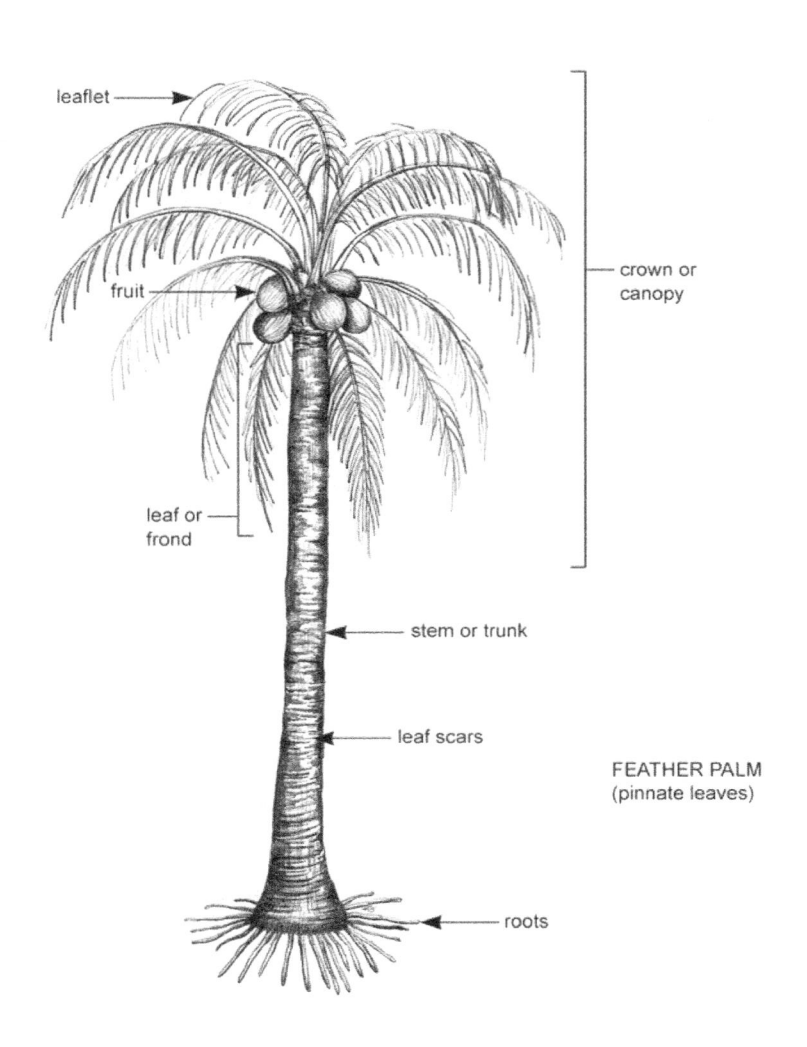

Leaves/ into the leaf/ fractal vibration
Look
into the fractal infinity.

The tree itself, a leaf.

Each branch, the tree.
And in all the veins,
a fractal of itself.

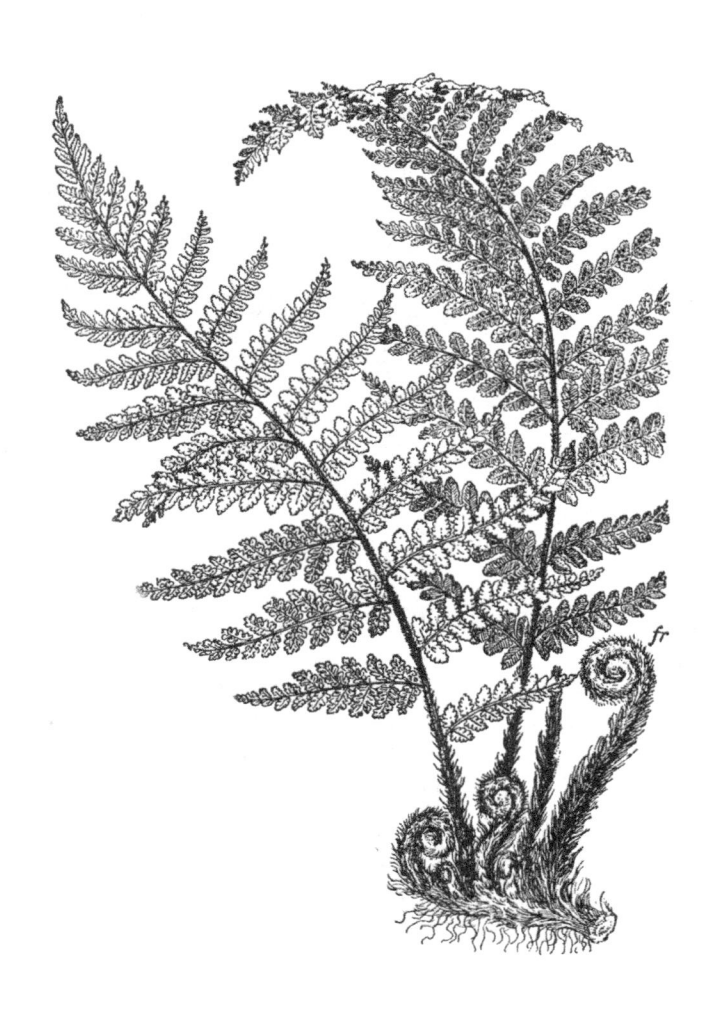

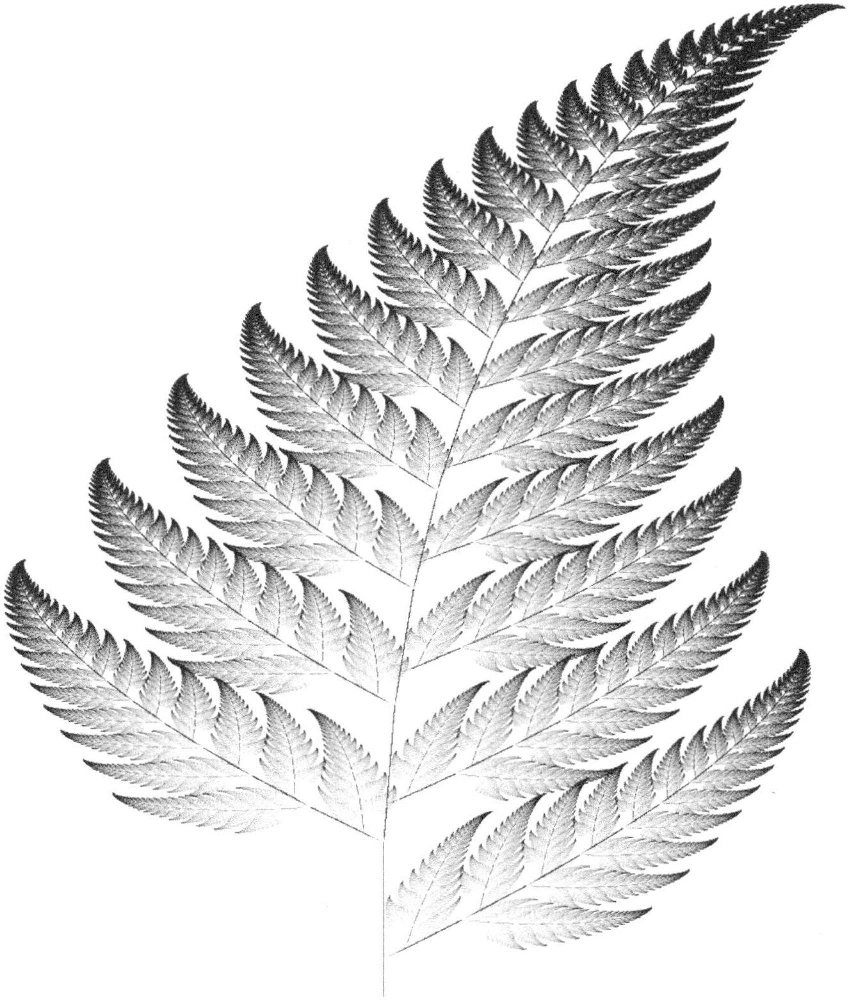

Root System

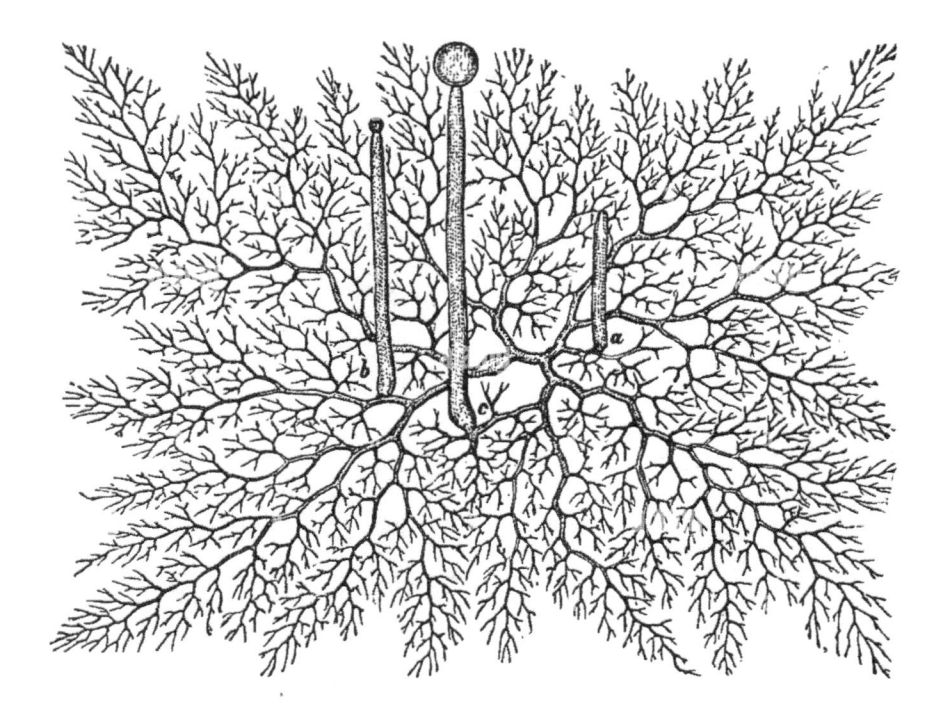

Shapes of God/ vegetables
Spines,
leveled and balance
like a stick in the mud.
Odd shapes
trying to become the sun.

Fingers, roots and limbs
studded in the resistance.

Blooming in the shapes of God.

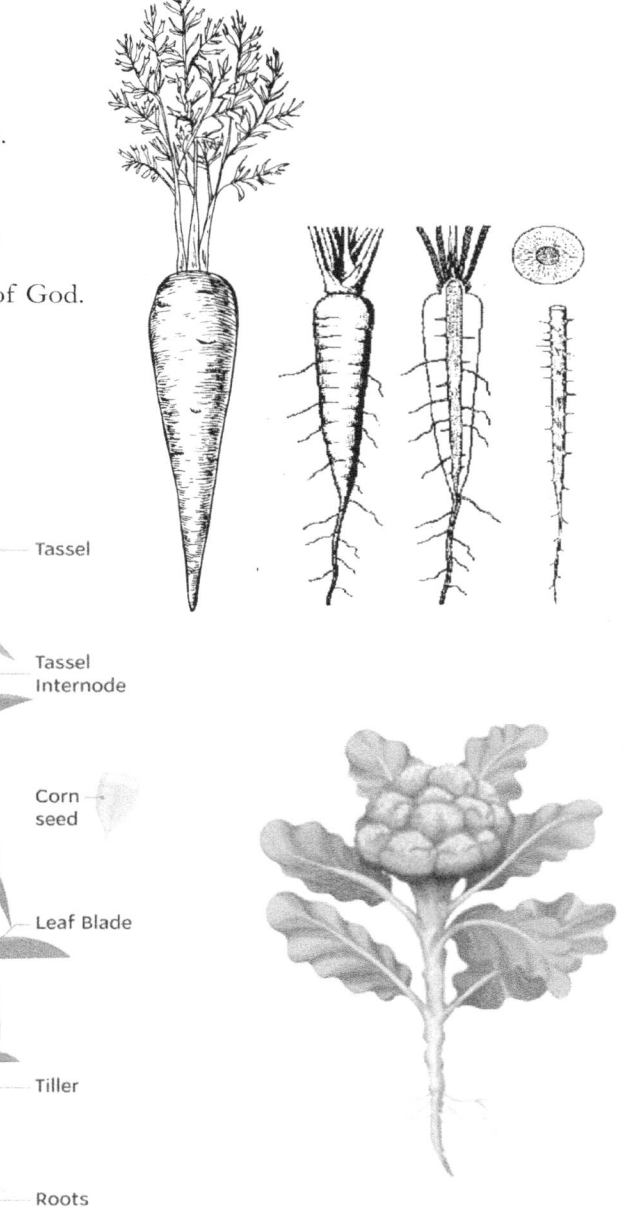

Nuts and Seeds

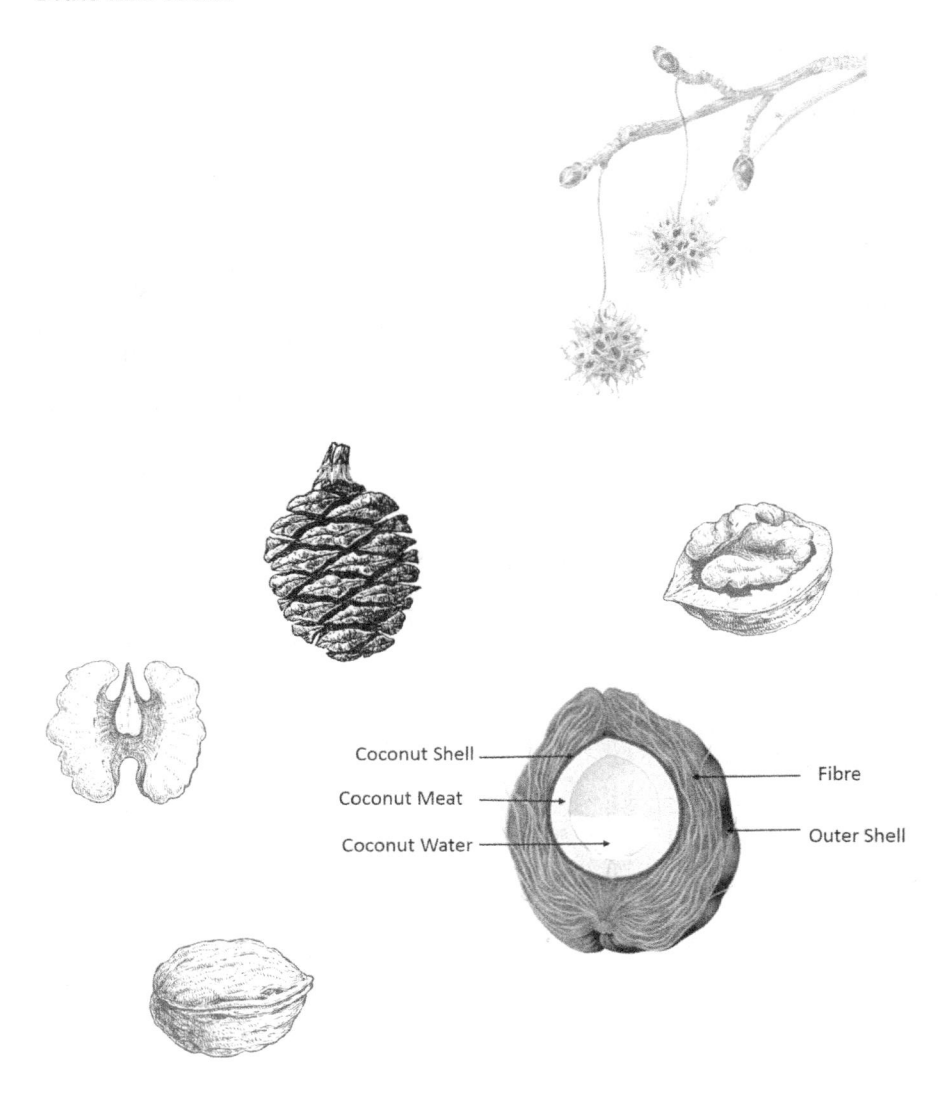

Coconut Shell — Fibre
Coconut Meat — Outer Shell
Coconut Water

Fruit of the Universe
See the stars;

The solar system
in the flesh and rind.

Potential.

Magnetic field pattern.

Infinity is the earth.

And forever will be,
fruit of the universe.

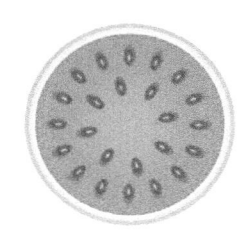

Flowers
At the tip of my root,
I take shape
of the snowflake

Radiate
out in pedals.

I am the sun
tied to soil.

Efficiency/ watering itself
Nature is efficient.

Spread,
curved leaves into funnel
to feed themselves.

Warming,
and watering itself.

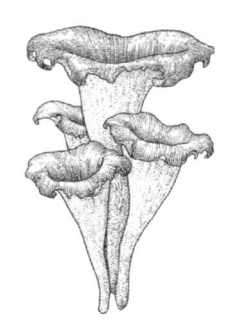

Ocean
Balanced,
is the water.

In a tame vibration
searching for rest.

And the planets, stars and moon,
are the winds,
fighting for its beauty.

Pushing, pulling,
tugging up and down
on the oceans waves.

Sea Floor/ sea creatures
Find creatures
in the shape of the sun.

On the sea floor,
veins and brains in coral.

Swirling tails
and sea shells,
in the shape of the falling universe.

Patterns of lightening.

Beings of the galaxy.

In fractals
floating through space.

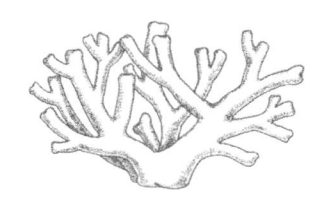

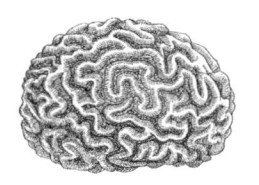

Enchanted Forest/ beauty of nature/ the heavenly garden
Enchanted,
is the existence around you.

The heavenly garden.

Humidity in the air,
and steam fills my lungs.

Animals run,
soar, swim
through the atom.

I find myself,
in the mystical forest that is life.

In it's luscious shapes and colour.

I will walk you through.

Introduce you;

To beauty

Trying to Become Conscious
By law of the universe,
the pattern of motion comes to life.

Everything
trying to become conscious.

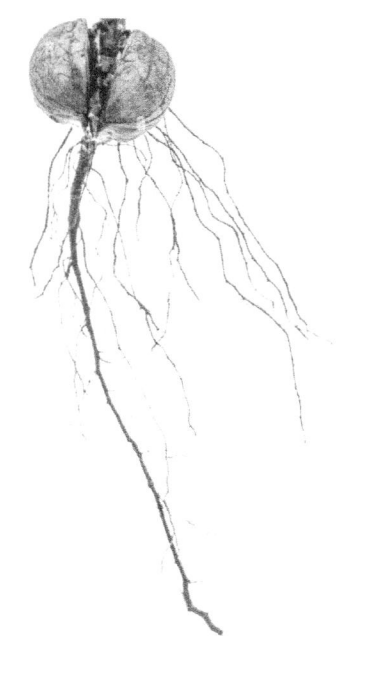

Suit of Armor/ body
Tissue and bone.

Muscle, skin and skull.

Overthrown by clothes.

Body in survival.

Heart and brain
with veins,
builds a suit of armor.

Protected
by the harsh substance
that is

reality.

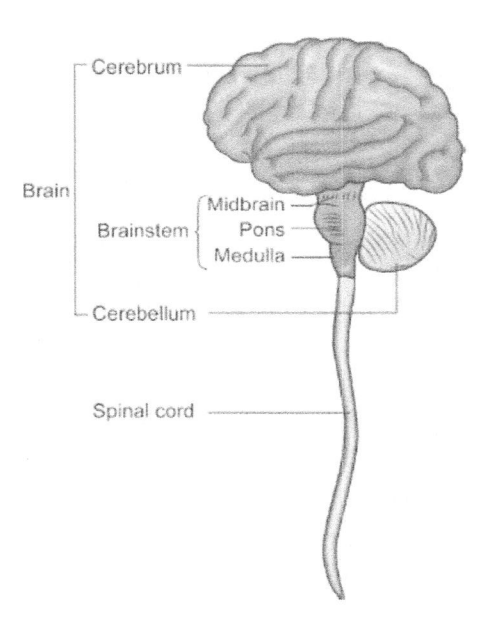

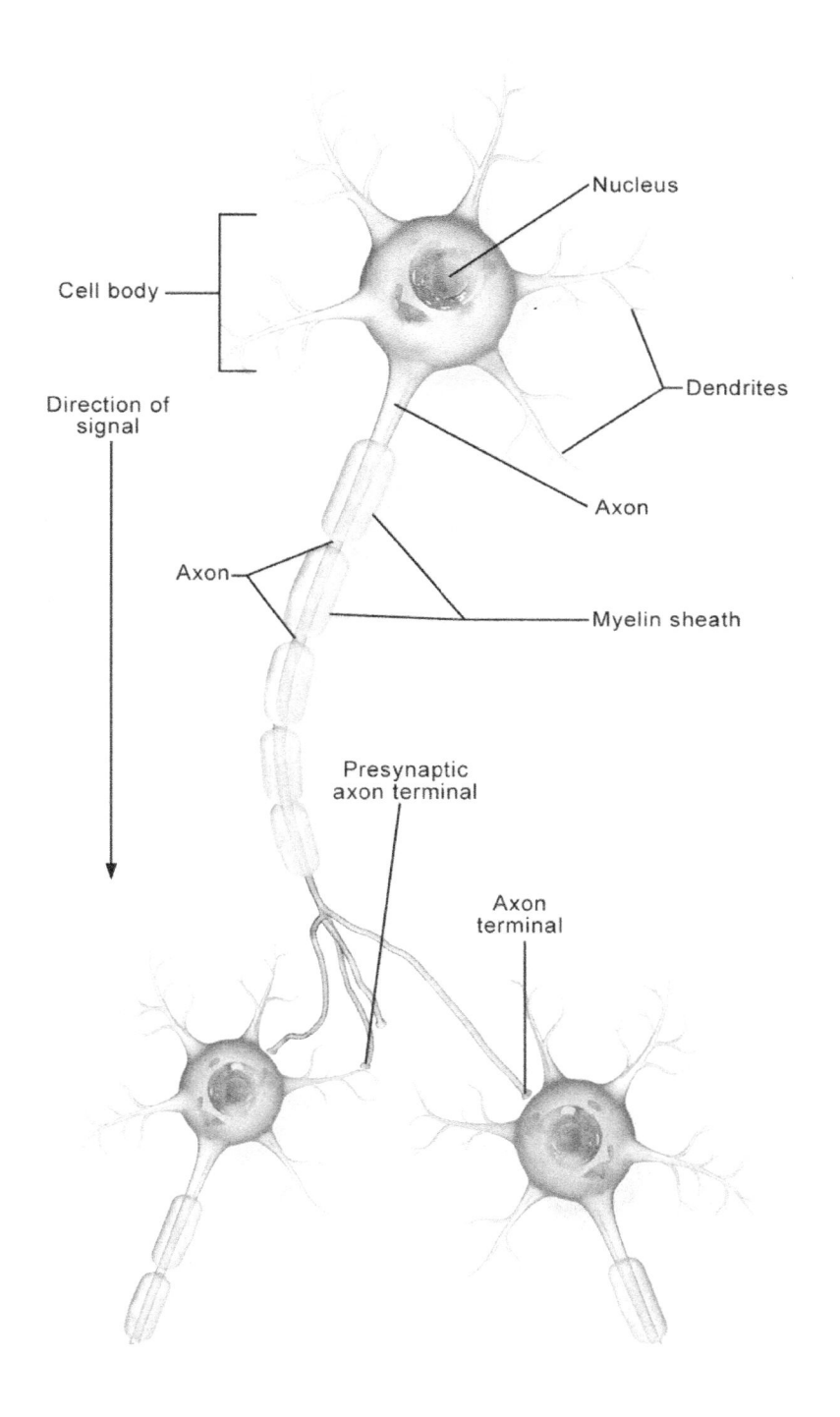

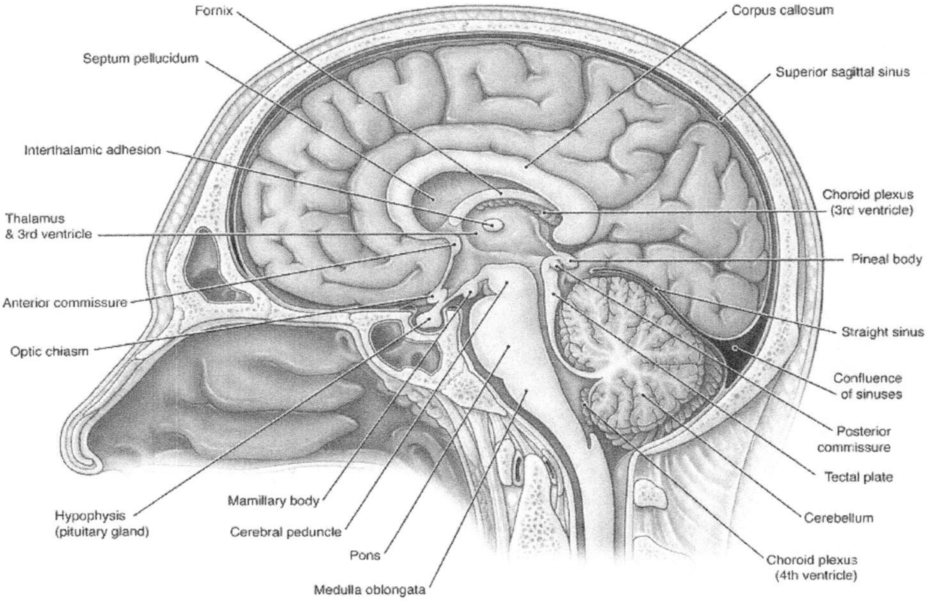
Fornix
Corpus callosum
Septum pellucidum
Superior sagittal sinus
Interthalamic adhesion
Choroid plexus
(3rd ventricle)
Thalamus
& 3rd ventricle
Pineal body
Anterior commissure
Straight sinus
Optic chiasm
Confluence
of sinuses
Posterior
commissure
Tectal plate
Cerebellum
Hypophysis
(pituitary gland)
Mamillary body
Cerebral peduncle
Pons
Medulla oblongata
Choroid plexus
(4th ventricle)

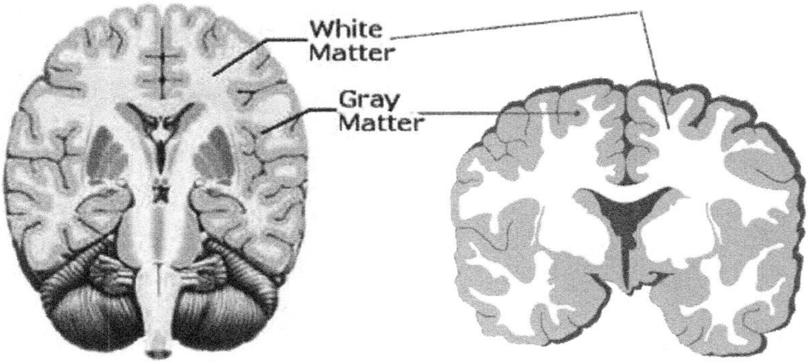
White
Matter
Gray
Matter

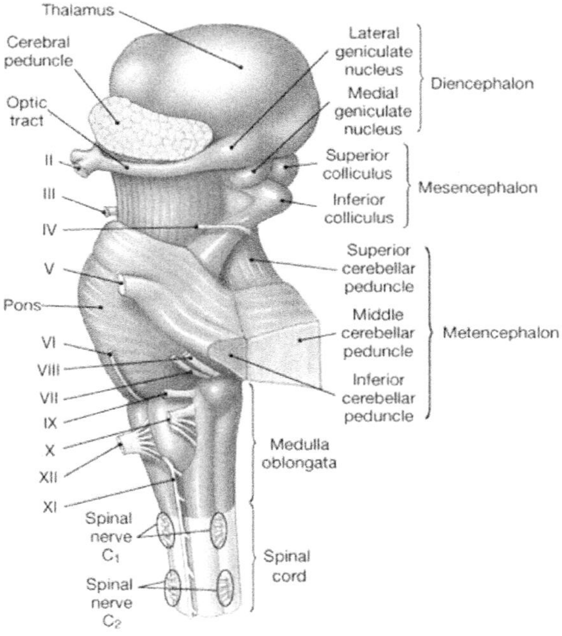

Thalamus
Cerebral peduncle
Optic tract
II
III
IV
V
Pons
VI
VIII
VII
IX
X
XII
XI
Spinal nerve C_1
Spinal nerve C_2
Lateral geniculate nucleus
Medial geniculate nucleus
Diencephalon
Superior colliculus
Inferior colliculus
Mesencephalon
Superior cerebellar peduncle
Middle cerebellar peduncle
Inferior cerebellar peduncle
Metencephalon
Medulla oblongata
Spinal cord

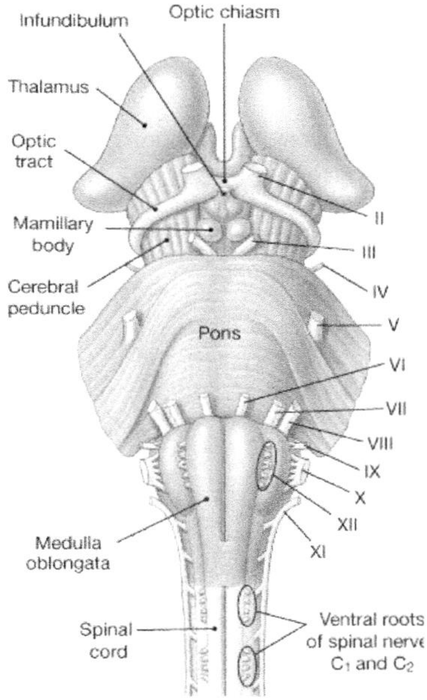

Infundibulum
Optic chiasm
Thalamus
Optic tract
Mamillary body
Cerebral peduncle
II
III
IV
V
Pons
VI
VII
VIII
IX
X
XII
XI
Medulla oblongata
Spinal cord
Ventral roots of spinal nerve C_1 and C_2

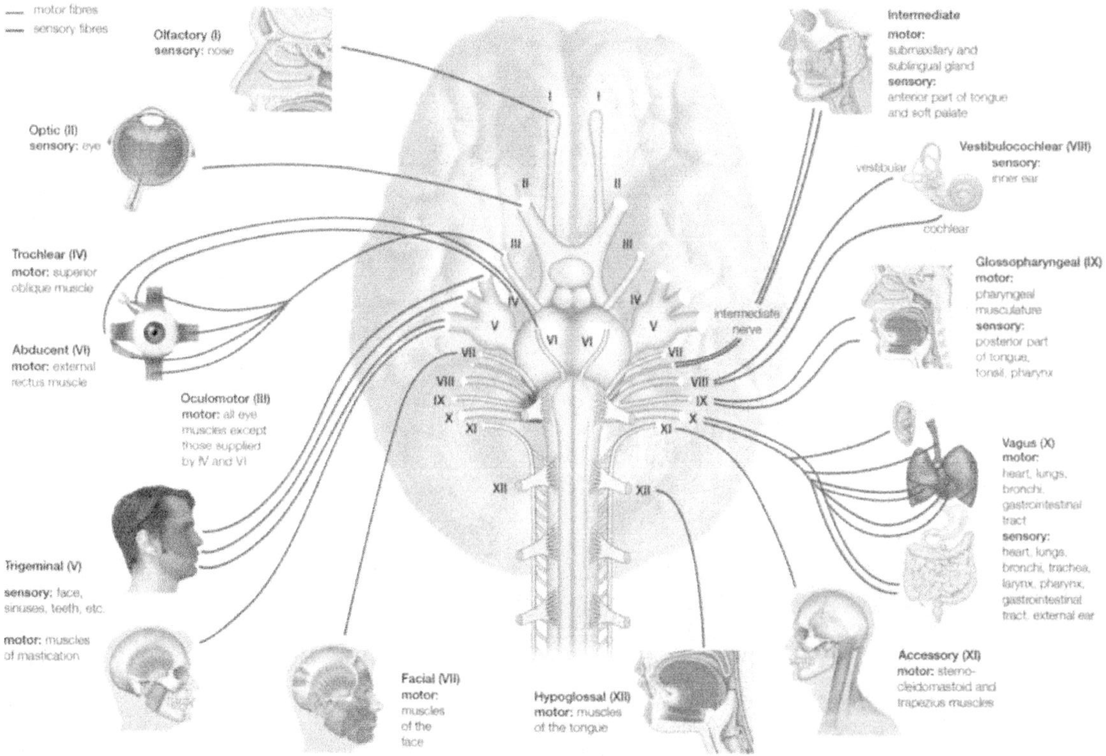

motor fibres
sensory fibres
Olfactory (I)
sensory: nose
Optic (II)
sensory: eye
Trochlear (IV)
motor: superior oblique muscle
Abducent (VI)
motor: external rectus muscle
Oculomotor (III)
motor: all eye muscles except those supplied by IV and VI
Trigeminal (V)
sensory: face, sinuses, teeth, etc.
motor: muscles of mastication
Facial (VII)
motor: muscles of the face
Hypoglossal (XII)
motor: muscles of the tongue
Accessory (XI)
motor: sterno-cleidomastoid and trapezius muscles
Vagus (X)
motor: heart, lungs, bronchi, gastrointestinal tract
sensory: heart, lungs, bronchi, trachea, larynx, pharynx, gastrointestinal tract, external ear
Glossopharyngeal (IX)
motor: pharyngeal musculature
sensory: posterior part of tongue, tonsil, pharynx
Vestibulocochlear (VIII)
sensory: inner ear
vestibular
cochlear
Intermediate
motor: submaxillary and sublingual gland
sensory: anterior part of tongue and soft palate
intermediate nerve
I
II
III
IV
V
VI
VII
VIII
IX
X
XI
XII

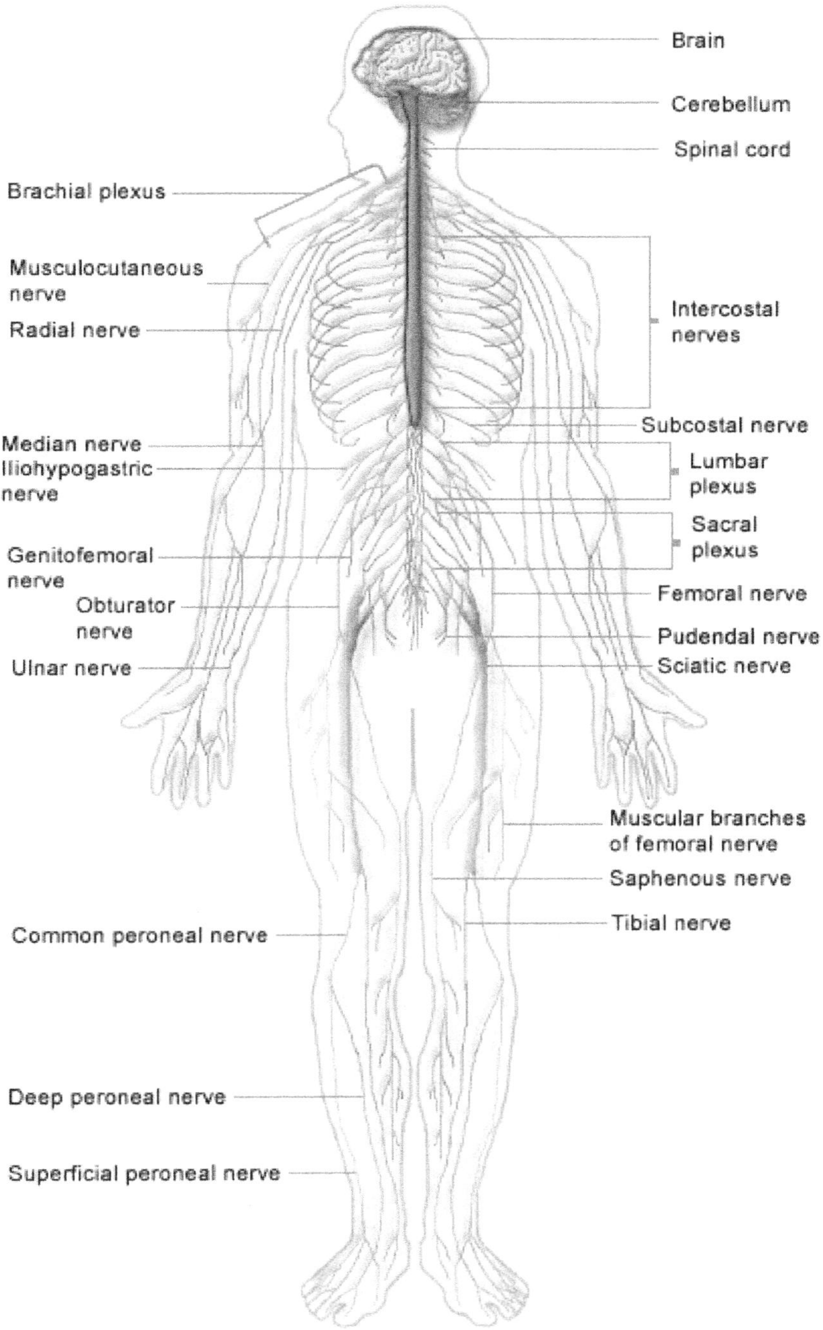
Brain
Cerebellum
Spinal cord
Brachial plexus
Musculocutaneous nerve
Radial nerve
Intercostal nerves
Subcostal nerve
Median nerve
Iliohypogastric nerve
Lumbar plexus
Sacral plexus
Genitofemoral nerve
Obturator nerve
Femoral nerve
Pudendal nerve
Ulnar nerve
Sciatic nerve
Muscular branches of femoral nerve
Saphenous nerve
Tibial nerve
Common peroneal nerve
Deep peroneal nerve
Superficial peroneal nerve

"Human"

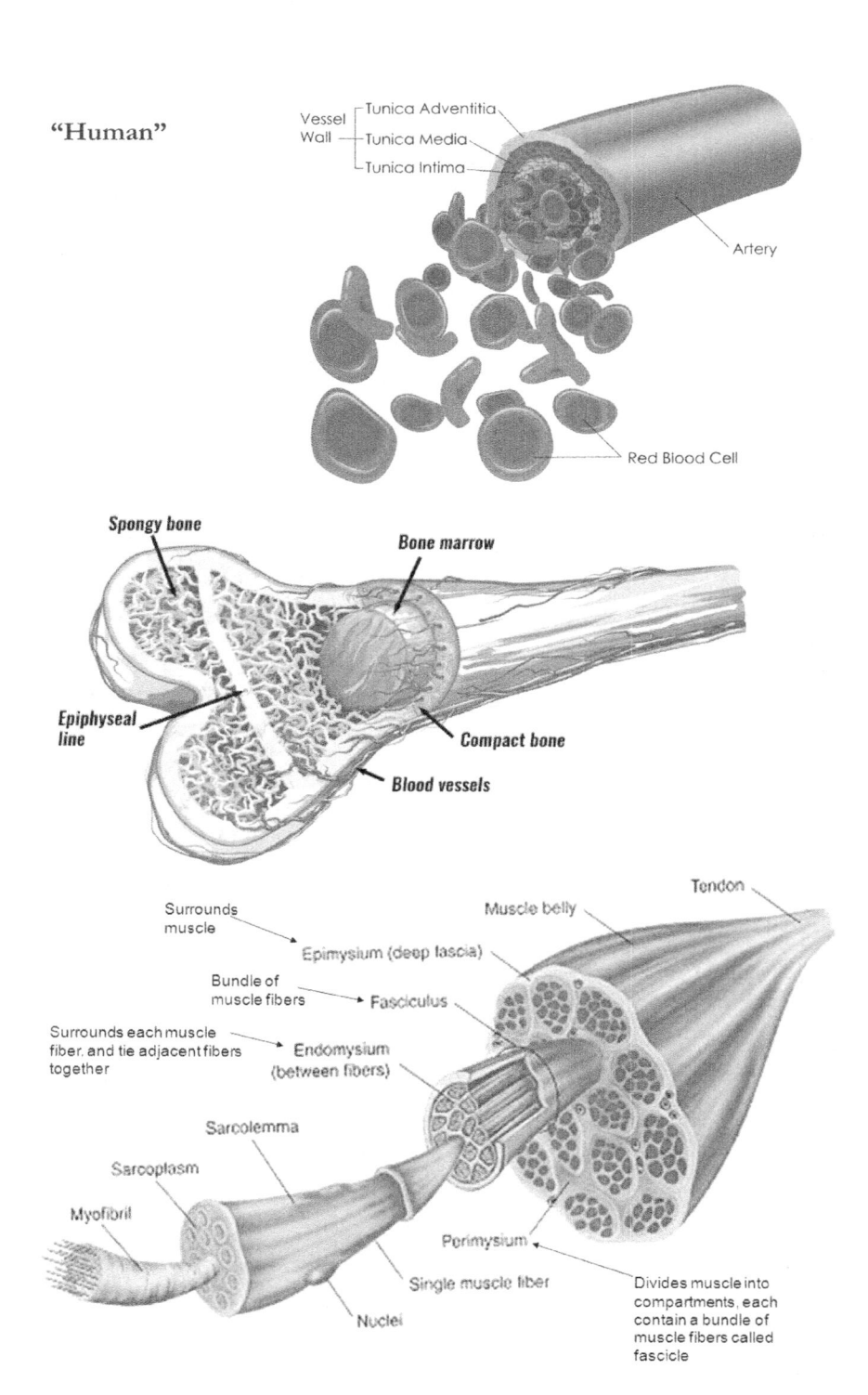

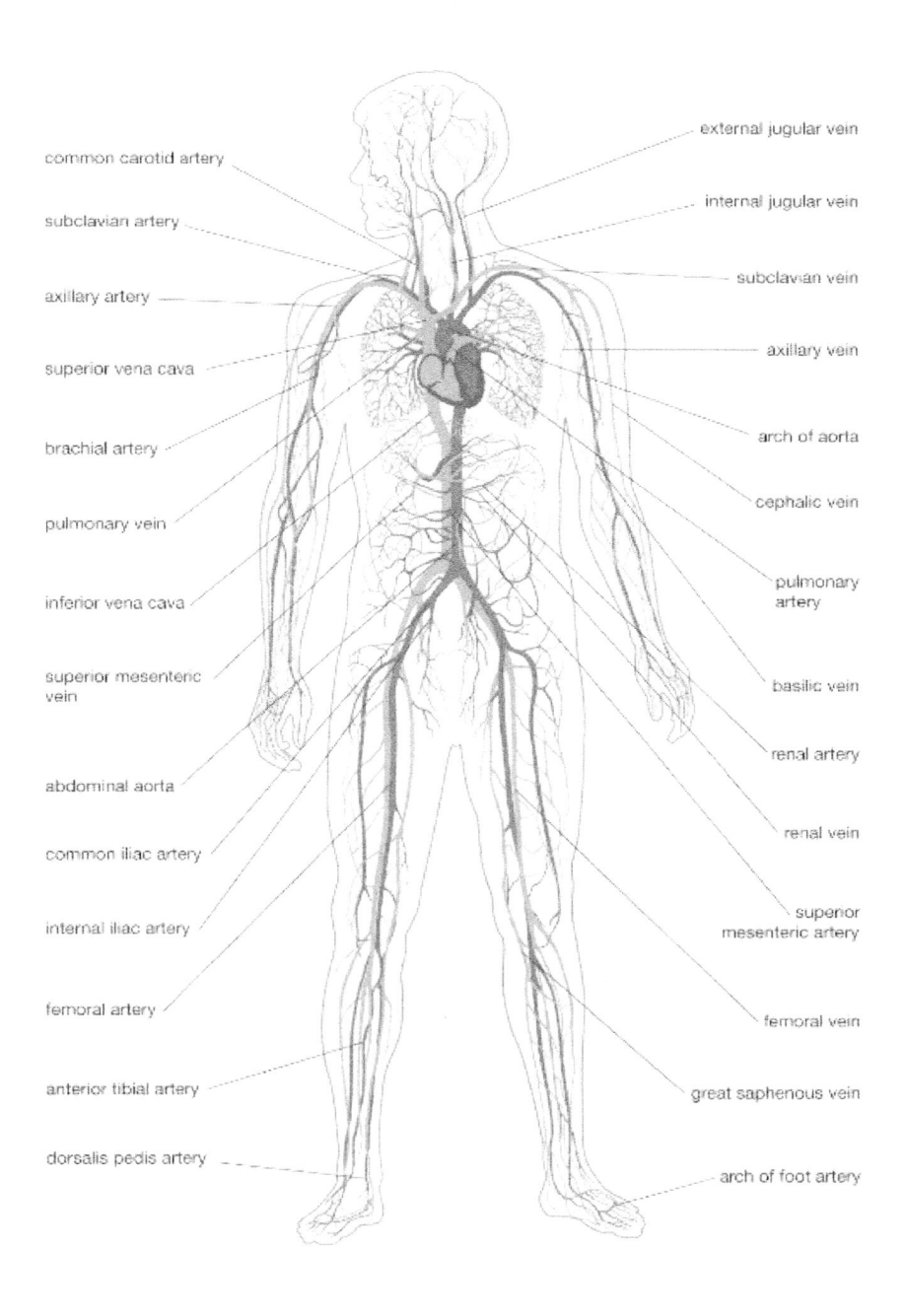

- common carotid artery
- subclavian artery
- axillary artery
- superior vena cava
- brachial artery
- pulmonary vein
- inferior vena cava
- superior mesenteric vein
- abdominal aorta
- common iliac artery
- internal iliac artery
- femoral artery
- anterior tibial artery
- dorsalis pedis artery
- external jugular vein
- internal jugular vein
- subclavian vein
- axillary vein
- arch of aorta
- cephalic vein
- pulmonary artery
- basilic vein
- renal artery
- renal vein
- superior mesenteric artery
- femoral vein
- great saphenous vein
- arch of foot artery

Skin/ touch
Skin.

My body is an efficient receiver
picking up signal.

I am a conductor.

Nerves of vibration.

Through touch,
I avoid pain
in order to survive.

Gravitate to that which brings pleasure.

Sensations, throughout my body.

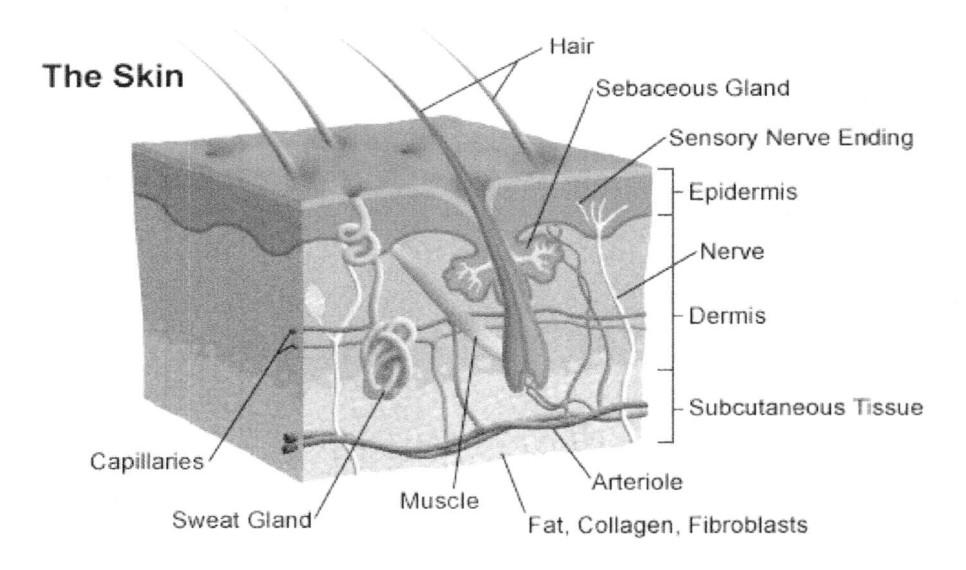

The Skin

- Hair
- Sebaceous Gland
- Sensory Nerve Ending
- Epidermis
- Nerve
- Dermis
- Subcutaneous Tissue
- Capillaries
- Sweat Gland
- Muscle
- Arteriole
- Fat, Collagen, Fibroblasts

Hair

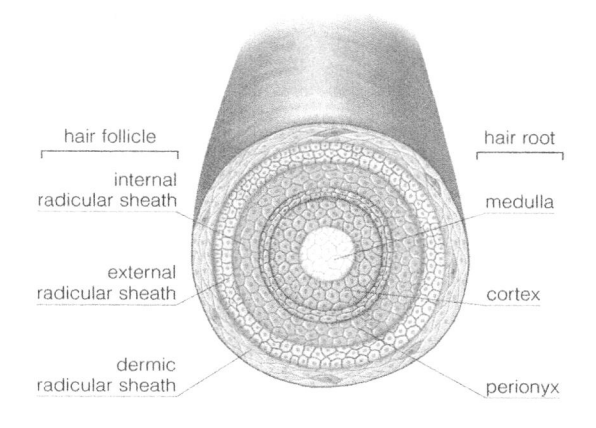

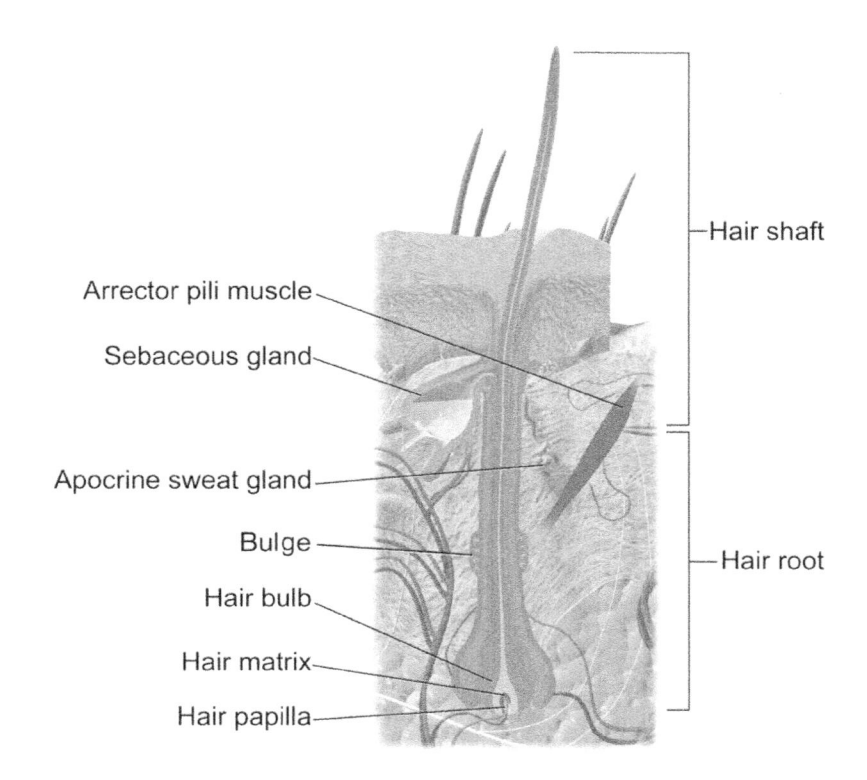

- hair follicle
  - internal radicular sheath
  - external radicular sheath
  - dermic radicular sheath
- hair root
  - medulla
  - cortex
  - perionyx

- Arrector pili muscle
- Sebaceous gland
- Apocrine sweat gland
- Bulge
- Hair bulb
- Hair matrix
- Hair papilla
- Hair shaft
- Hair root

Hearing/ ears

I hear the matter.
I am alert.

There is a difference in vibrations of tone.

Listening for screams;
or poetry.

Cries
touching the thin skin
of my ear drum,
and I come,
or go
running.

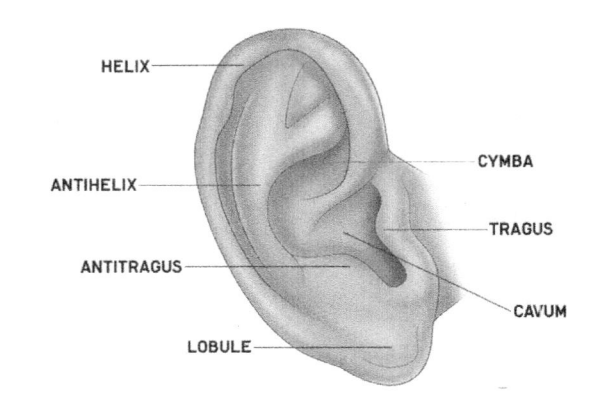

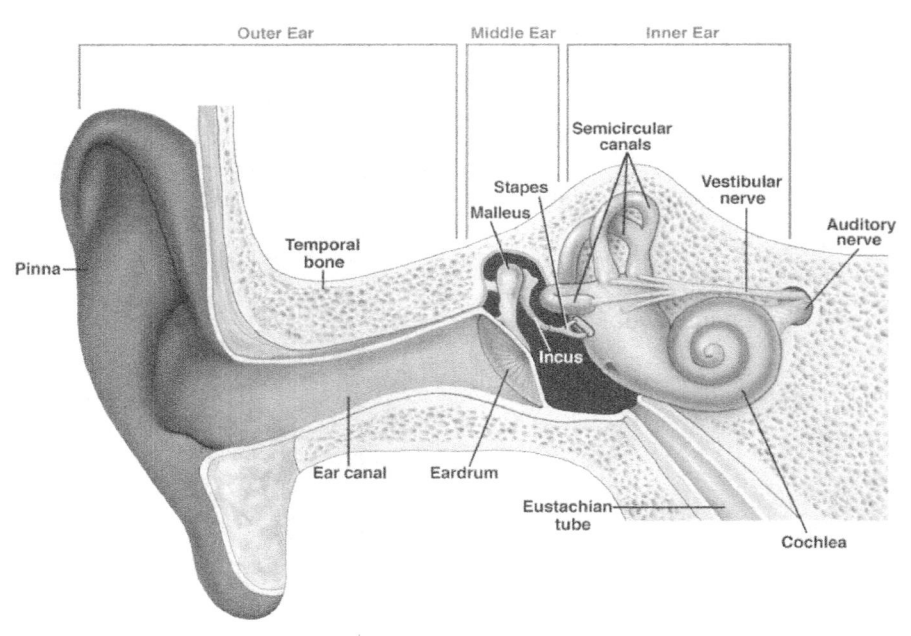

Smell/ senses
There is a smell in the air.

Rotting, or fresh.

Something to consume,
or death.

And my senses guide me.

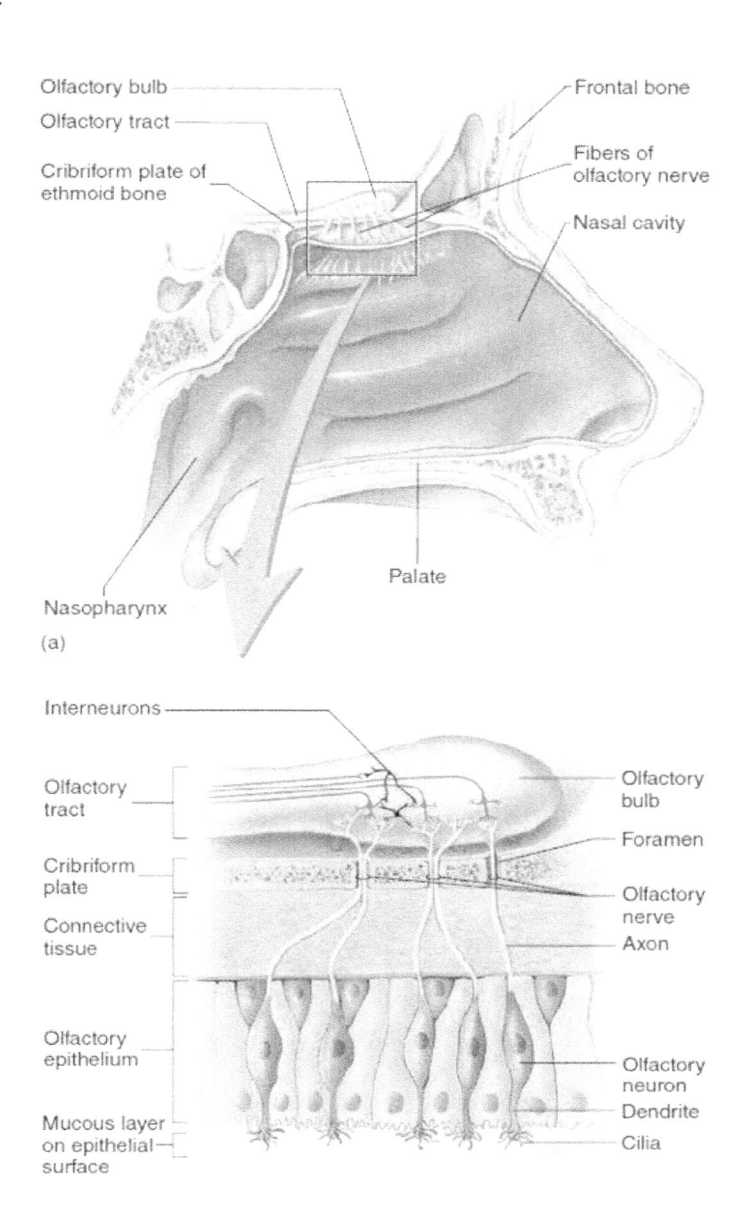

Olfactory bulb
Olfactory tract
Cribriform plate of ethmoid bone
Frontal bone
Fibers of olfactory nerve
Nasal cavity
Palate
Nasopharynx
(a)

Interneurons
Olfactory tract
Cribriform plate
Connective tissue
Olfactory epithelium
Mucous layer on epithelial surface
Olfactory bulb
Foramen
Olfactory nerve
Axon
Olfactory neuron
Dendrite
Cilia

Taste/mouth

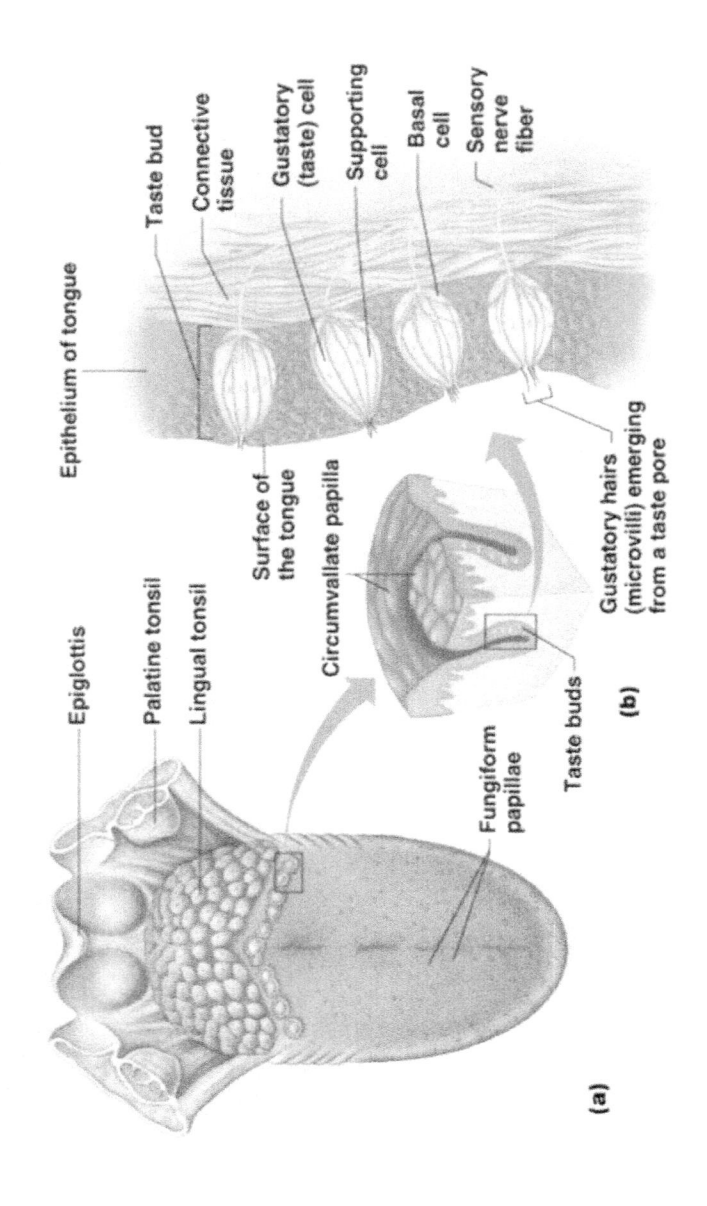

Sight
You are fundamental.

The eye.

The conscious being
observing everything.

Look around,
at heaven before you.

See the universe reflecting back.

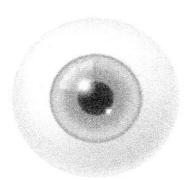

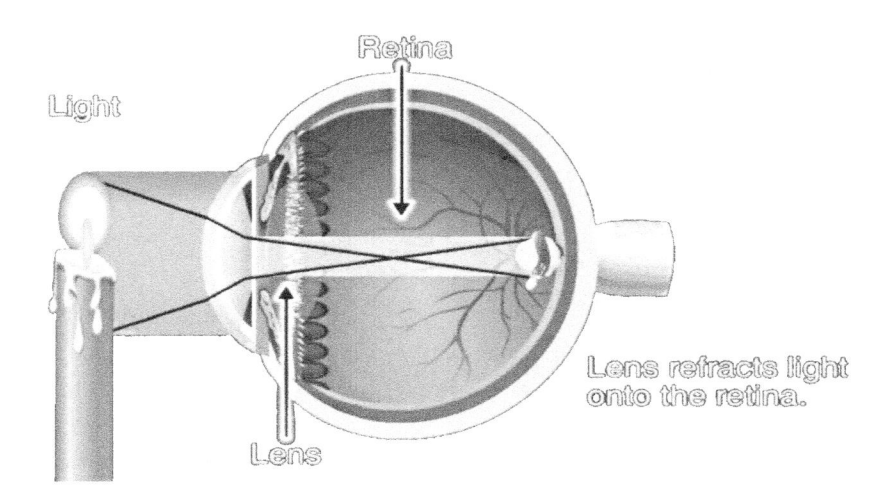

Lens refracts light onto the retina.

Find the Universe in Me/ the great all
I contain earth,
the stars,
the infinite.

Mechanics of the great all.

Find the universe in me.

Layered in perfect chemistry.

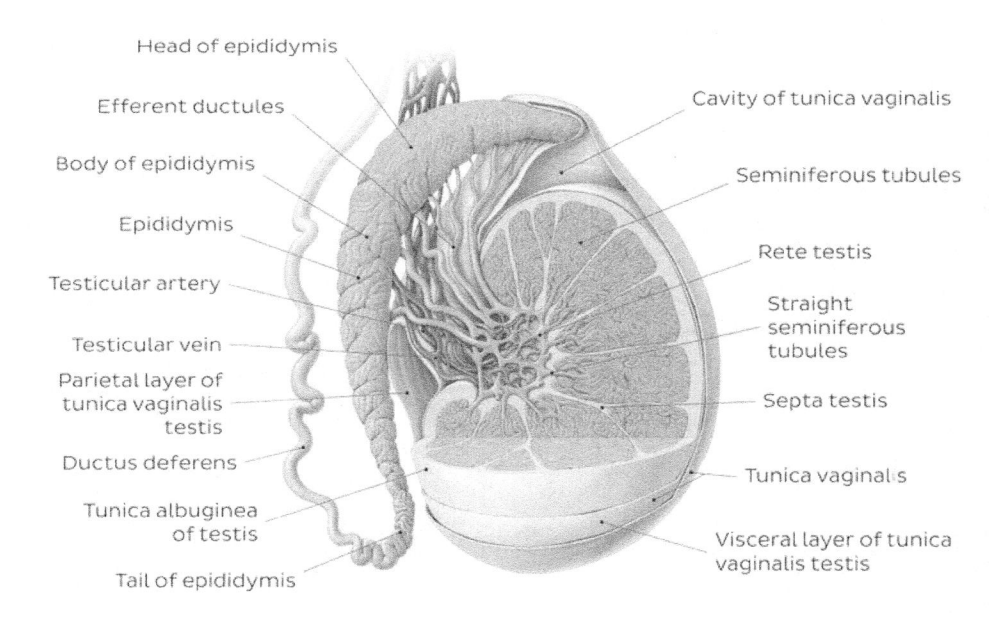

Reproductive Organ

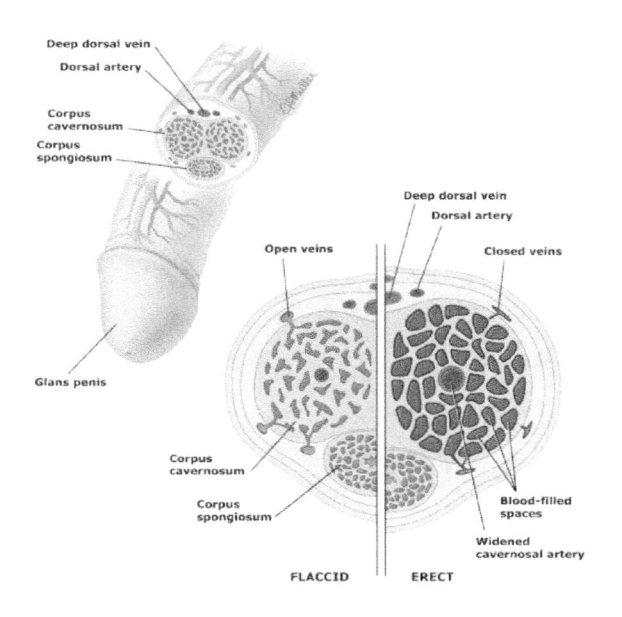

Heartbeat/ born

We are the pulsing fire.

The heart beat.

The electric shock,

deep within the universe.

Waiting
to be born.

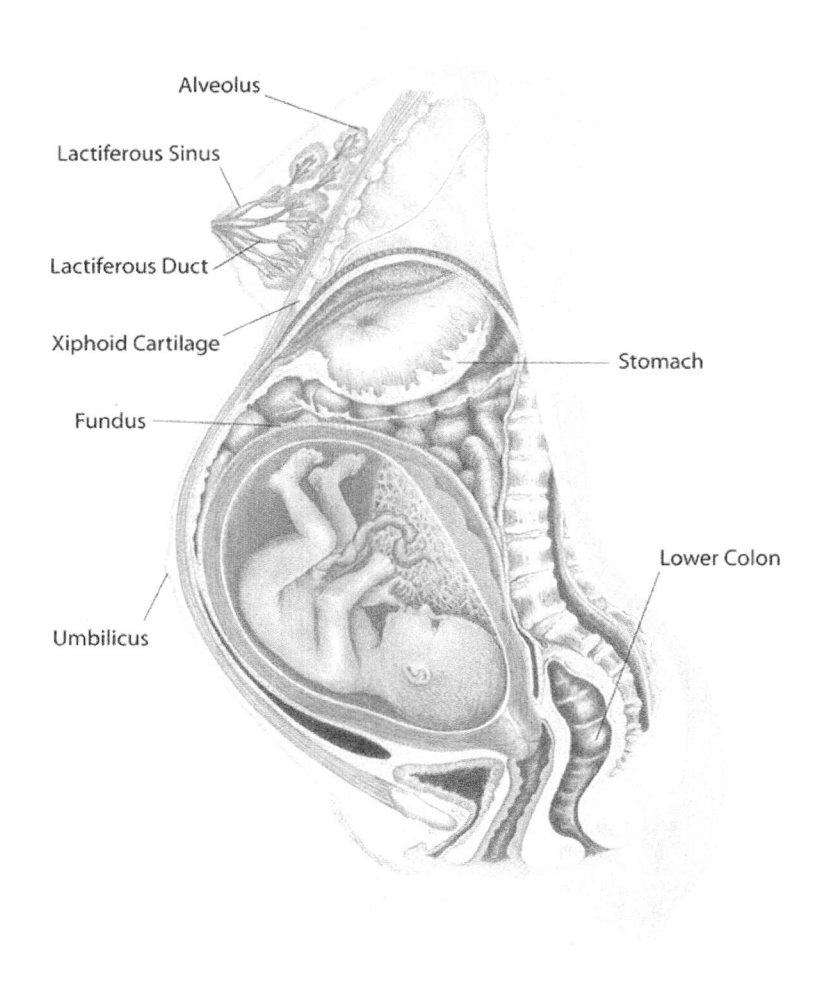

Chapter 3: God of Writing/ ether

The Great Unification/ the potential universe
The great unification

Trapped,
bound by the infinite.

Potential.

One energy.

One phenomenon.

One reality.

One entity.

One happening.

One presence.

One truth.

As you are it.

No death,
nor separation.

There is no escaping the atom
and the eternal oneness of existence.

What Man Calls/ god/ energy/ light/ space/ the universe/ the sphere/ the elements/ colour, shape, sound
That
which you call elements;

Weather;

The storm and sun.

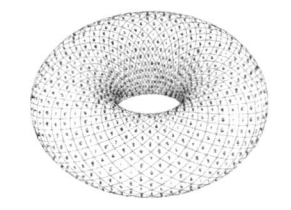

That
which you have called the sphere.

Colour, shape and sound.

That which moves.

That
which is infinite.

Acceleration;
The universe.

A system;

Toroidal opposition.

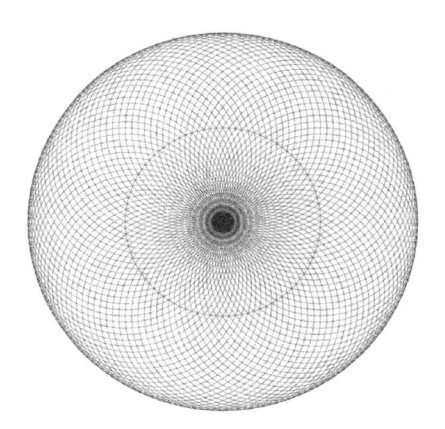

A field of existence.

And the conscious
to question and conquer.

Nature/ reality and perspective
All that is,
is nature.

What it is made of,
how it works.

Its existence
and possibilities;

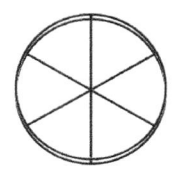

Reality and perspective

The conscious
lost in oneself.

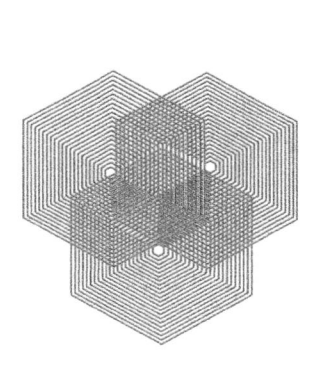

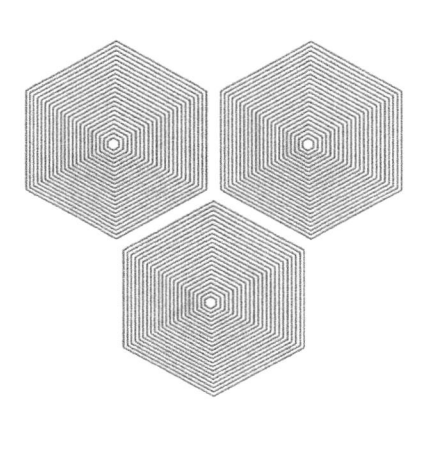

Law/ that which is happening/ physics
The absolute.

Applied here
and applied there.

What stands.

What is.

Applied to everything.

Law.

Forever will be.

Never to change.

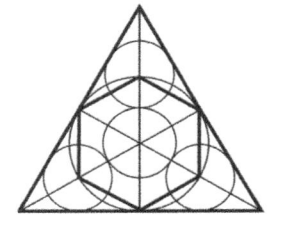

The Geometry of Motion and Structure/ throw

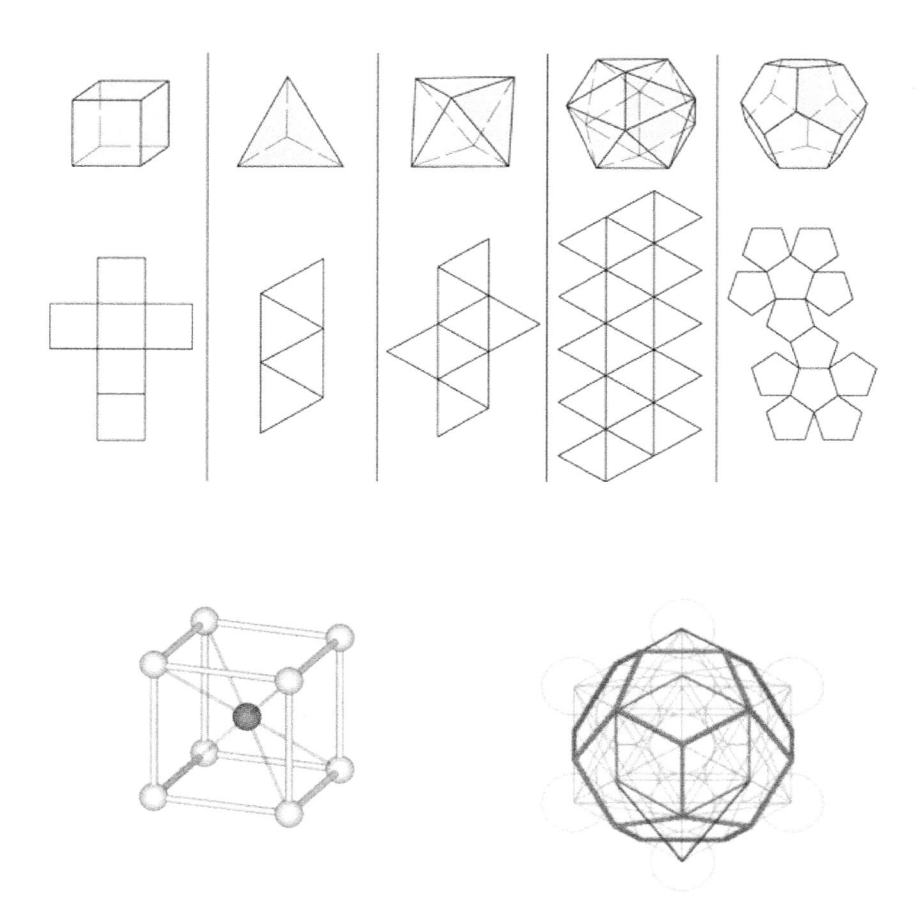

Crystals, Magnets, Electricity/ plant/ solar system/ dna/ universe/ what man has given name
The phenomenon;
induction, capacitance,
discharge, resistance

Magnetic,
electric.

Attributes of the all.

Be in awe,

at the crystal universe,
eroding, and falling.

Plants
solar system,
lightening, dna.

sharing the *one*
cosmic mechanic.

All man has given name.

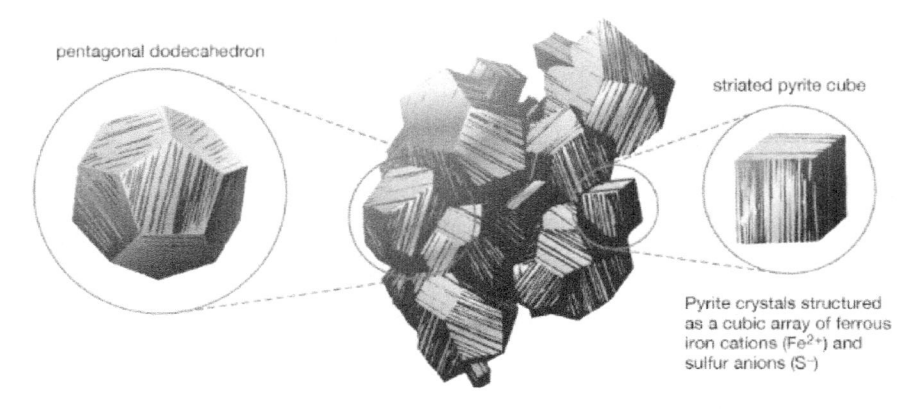

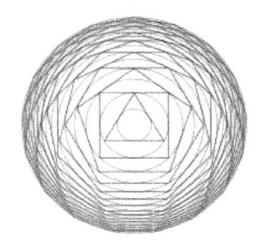

pentagonal dodecahedron

striated pyrite cube

Pyrite crystals structured as a cubic array of ferrous iron cations (Fe^{2+}) and sulfur anions (S^-)

Moving Stars/ the hollow moving star
Roaring stars
share their secret.

Star in stars.

Suns inside suns.

Allow in this knowledge
of the hollow *one*.

Geometry
of the sphere and ring.

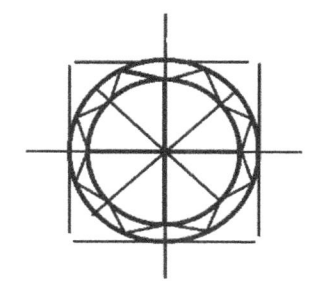

A fractal system
of stars moving.

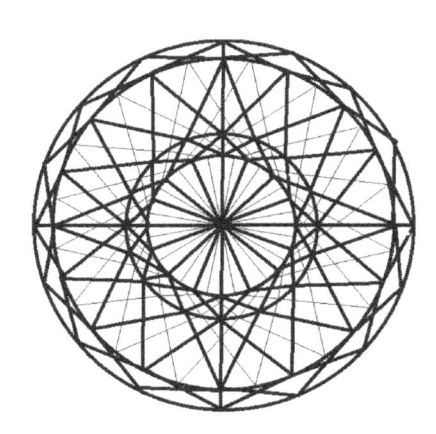

Substantial/ mass/ magnetic/ electric
Stars
share a little bit of themselves.

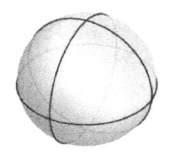

Substantial existence
that make up reality.

All physical,
are the sands
and trees.

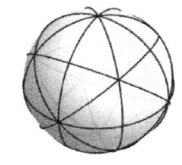

Mass,
magnetic.

Ripping and roaring into,
and as the universe.

Deteriorating rust.

planets and dust
are us.

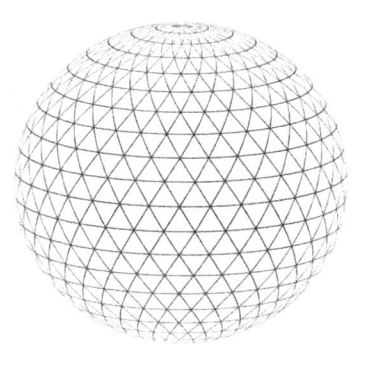

The Fractal Infinite/ mark of the fruit
Efficiently,
catching heat and moisture.

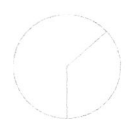

Feathered out distance furthest
of another.

Sharing the substance.

Equally.

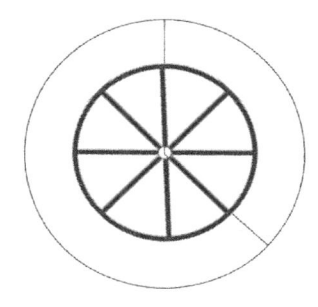

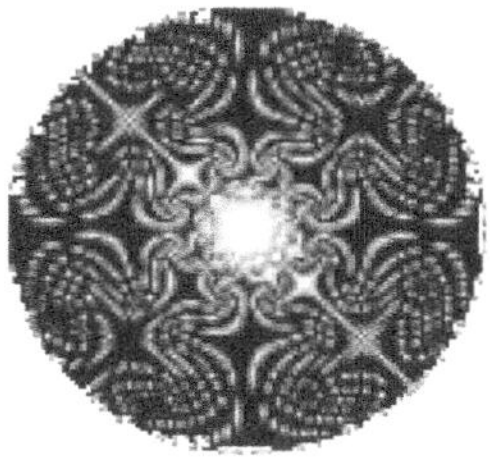
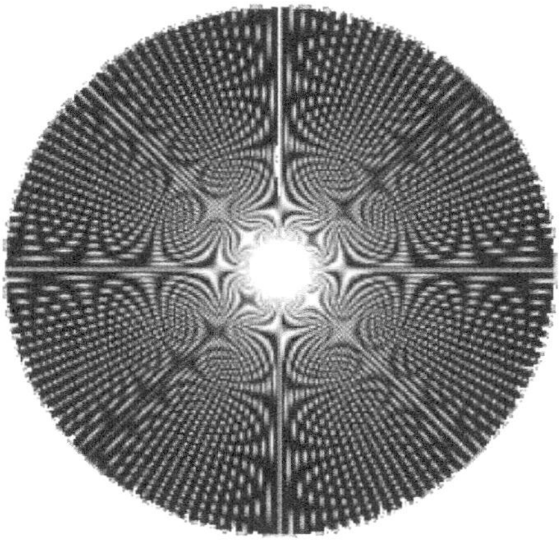
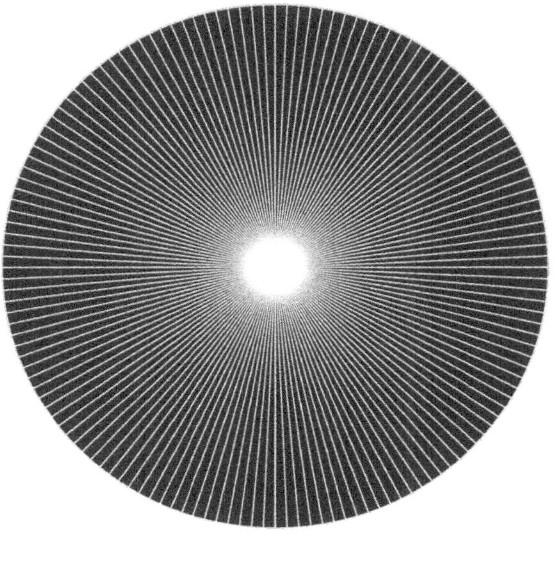

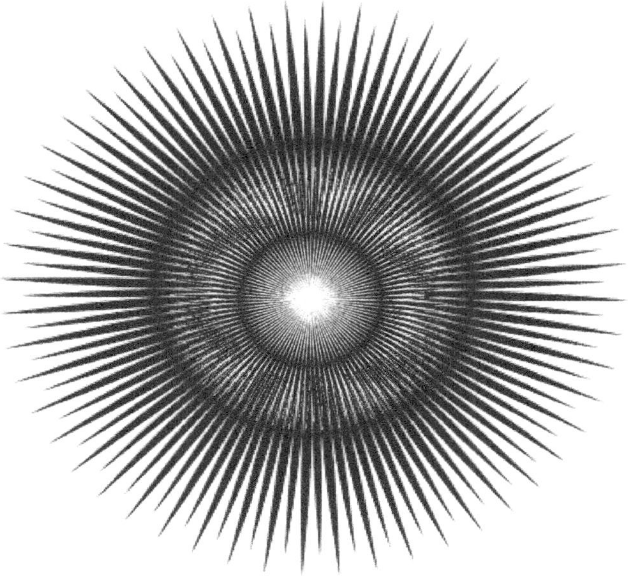

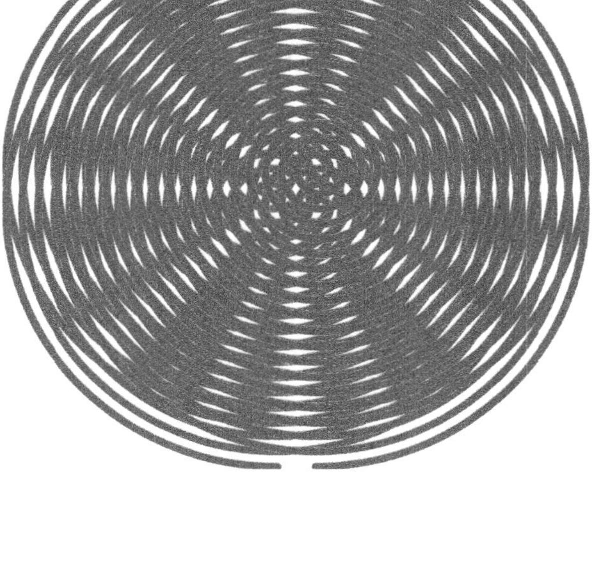

The Potential Field/ inside the fabric
Nature speaks.

A disturbance.

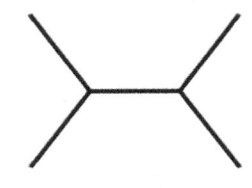

A rip
and compression
in the cosmos.

Inside the fabric,

a fractal reality.

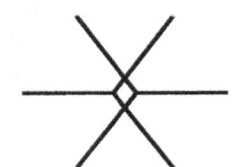

The potential field.

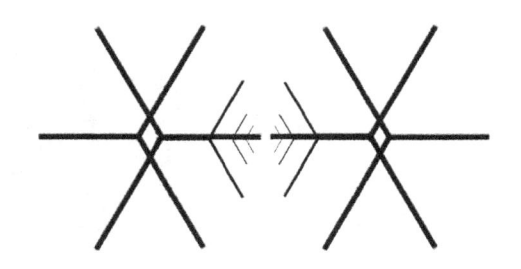

Path of Least Resistance / the efficient path

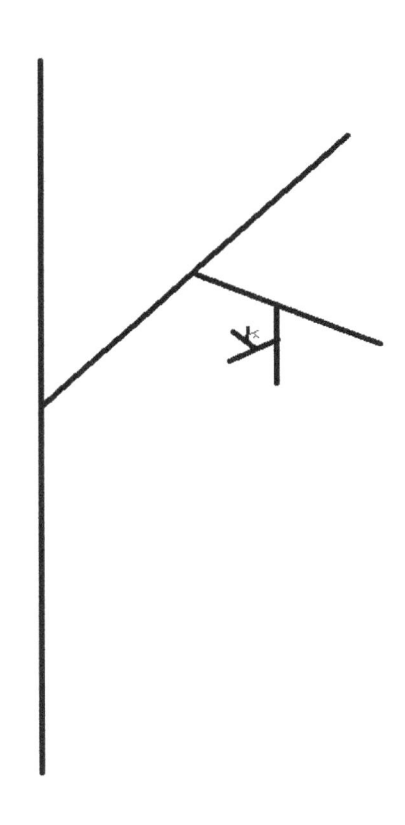

Winding Universe/ unwinding universe
The universe is opening,

closing
in an acceleration.

Tightening,
loosening

Folding,
and unfolding
in repeating fractals.

A vortex of memory.

Winding
and unwinding potential.

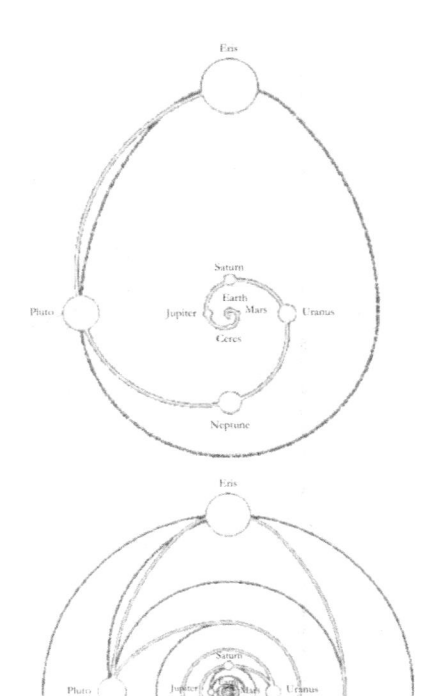

Interference/ the electric and magnetic/ electric, dielectric

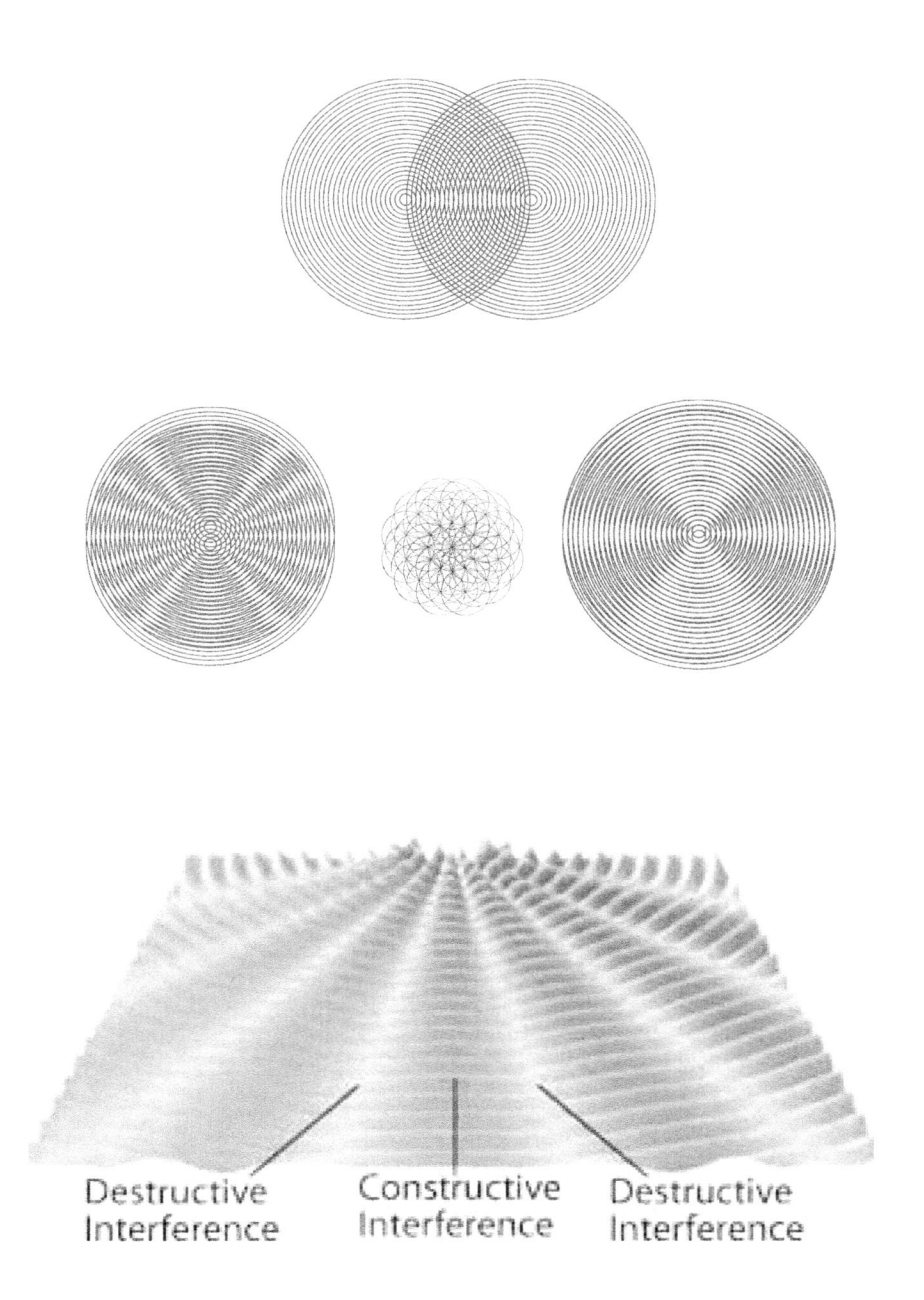

Destructive Interference   Constructive Interference   Destructive Interference

Magnetic Field/ electric field/defining the field/ torus field/ defining the star/ the universal system/ rotating/ accelerating universe/ the definition of energy/ mechanic of law/ ether field

Inside a magnet;

A cool spot,
in the flame.

Everything in everything;

A chamber of infinity.

Rings in rings.

Without center.

Null space potential energy.

Acceleration toward the lesser.

The magnetic;

The electric
thinning the fabric.

Fractals of iron and hydrogen.

Clashing, vibrating, melting,
burning and cooling.

Metal falling through air.

Inner, Outer Space/ inside, outside the fabric/ motion in opposition

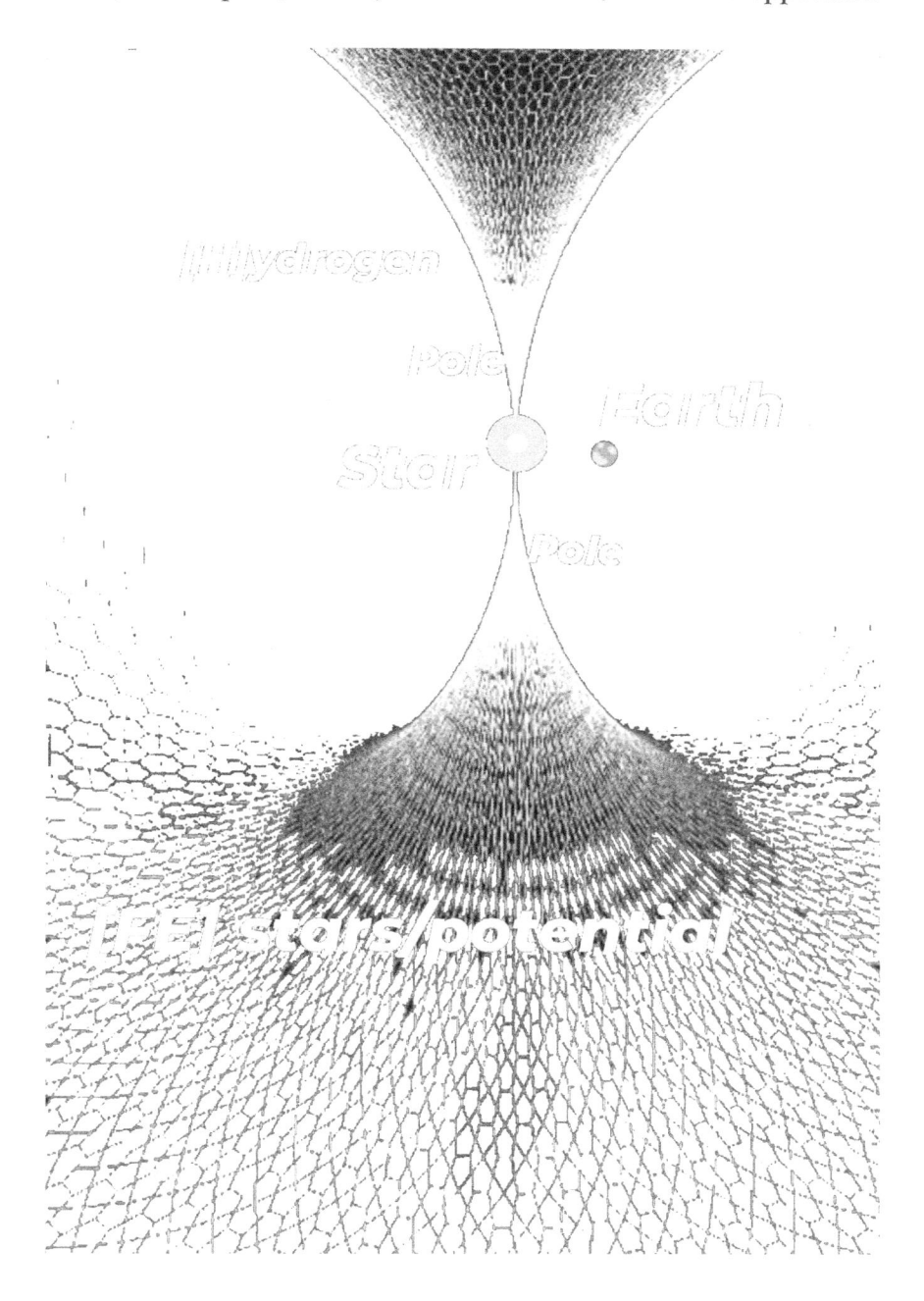

Stars and Shadow/ hot spot, cool spot
I stand
in the universal core.

Inside the firmament.

A dome of fire,

static, flame.

Walls of the system.

Bright stars.

The shell,
shining in the greater shadow.

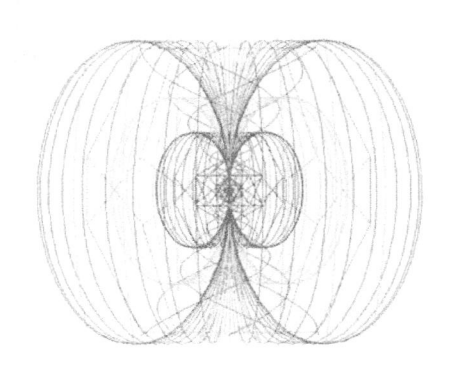

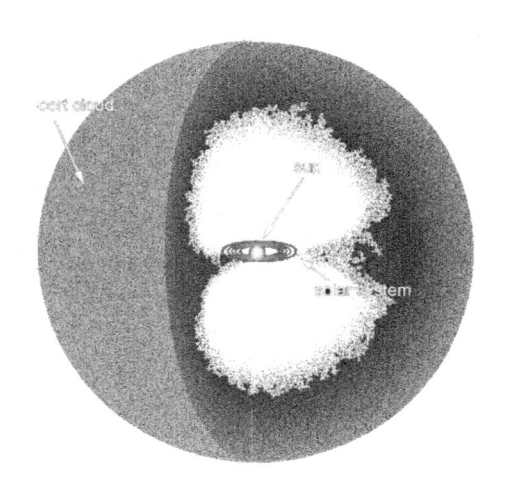

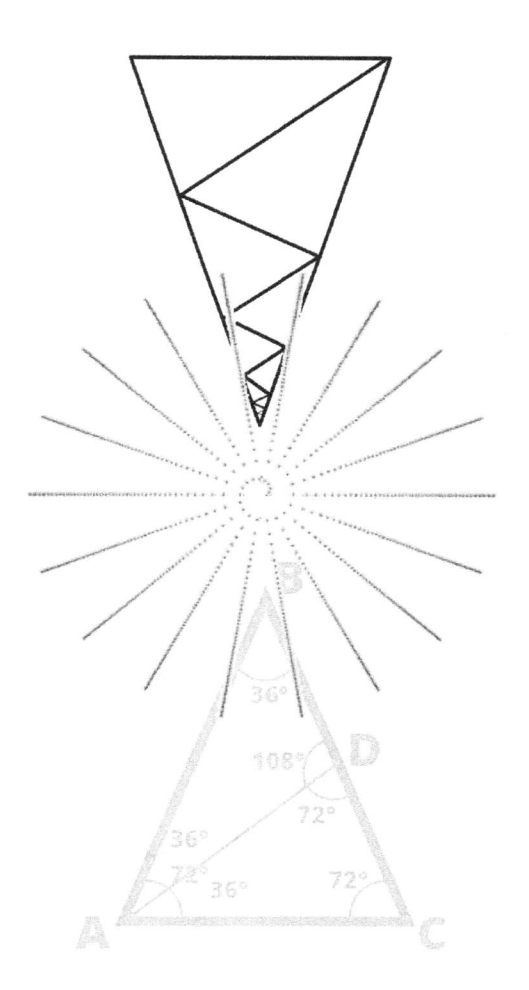

Potential Precession
The torus
wobbles and whirls.

As it rusts,
storms,
evaporates and strikes,
it breathes.

Absolute,
pure potential precession.

Spinning,

Dances around the sun.

And it,
around the galaxy.

Infinitely coiling.

In,
and around
the entire universe.

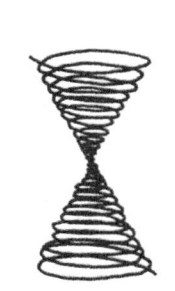

Perspective of the Ether/ the air
You are standing,
far too far,
and close to make any sense
of the full painting.

Beyond perspective.

See the universe,
a speck of dust in the air;

Only a piece of the great ether.

A block of salt in the ocean.

A grain in the sand.

A seed buried in soil

Comet in the galaxy

A planet in a shadow.

A flicker
in the dome of outer space.

Stars in the universe

Whirling with the wind.

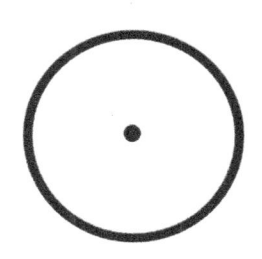

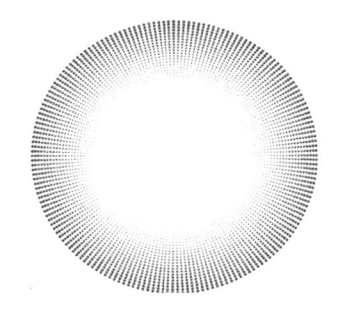

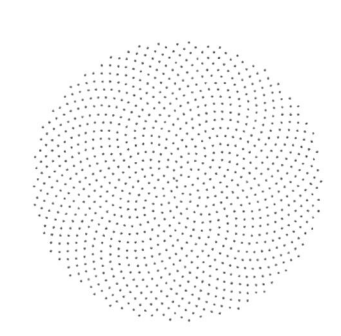

The Many Names and Perspective of Space/ witness the ether

Blooming,
eroding,
erupting,
raining.

Growing.

Flaming.
Floating.
Falling.

Spinning, folding,
sprouting.

All the same.

Witnessed
in perspective.

A happening

Infinity
stretched and compressed.

Spread
in all directions.

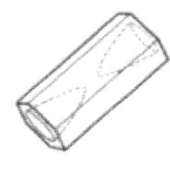

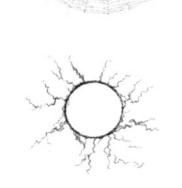

Coils, coils, coils/ coiling universe

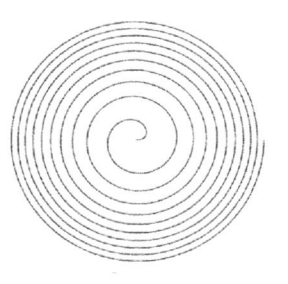

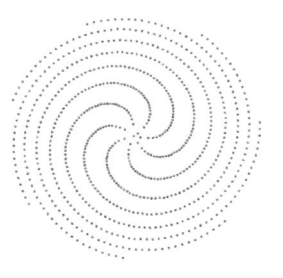

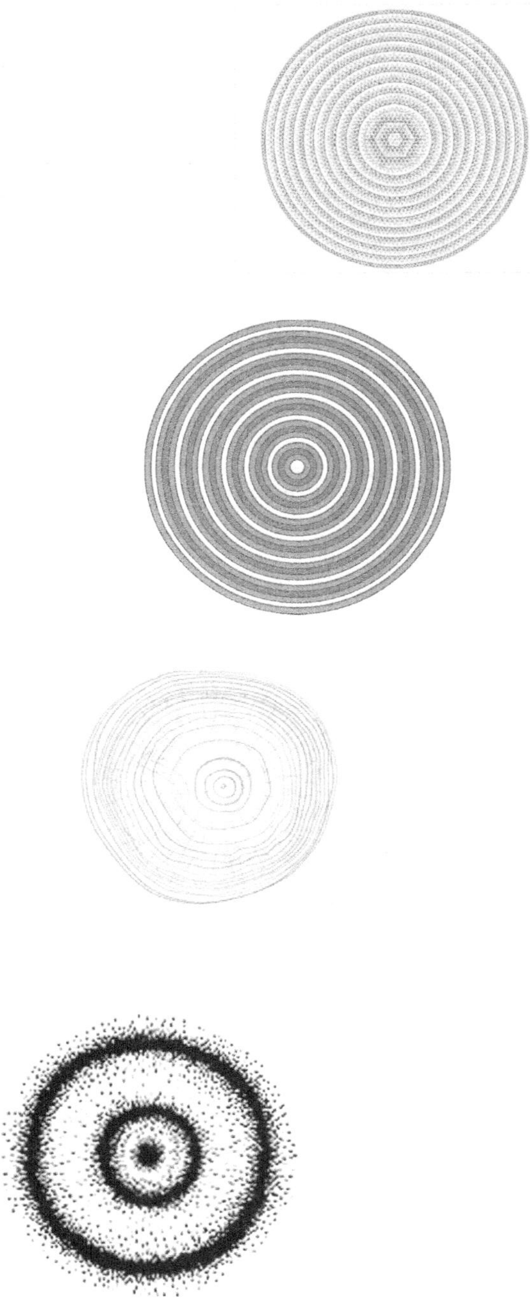

Star, Belt, Planet, Moon/ latitude, longitude
As belt is to sun,
so planet, disk, moon.

Latitude and longitude.

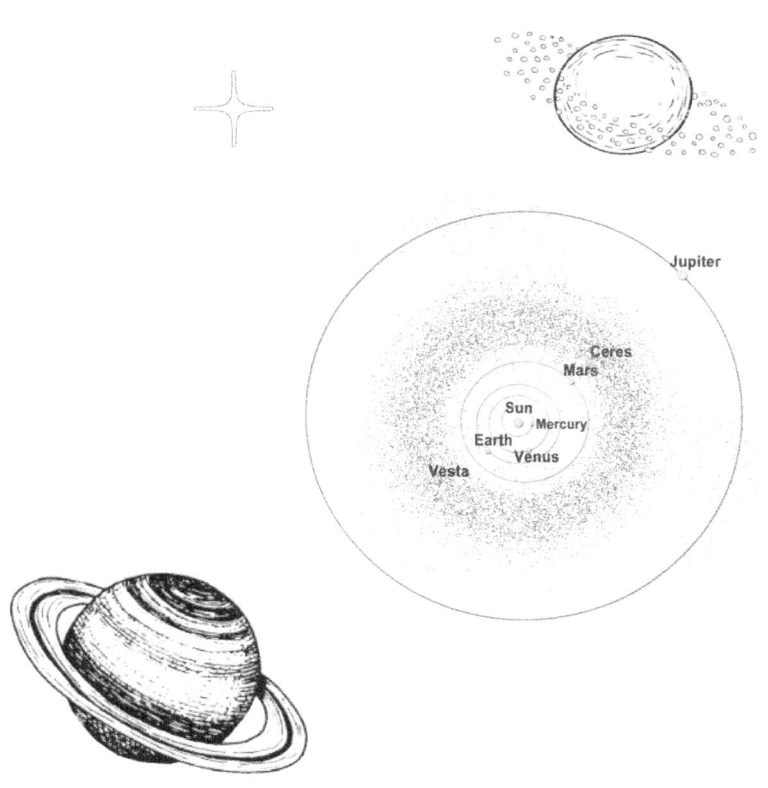

Sound is the Universe / music
Compressed sound
is all you've ever walked upon.

All is body.

All is the universe

All mind,
all music.

Disturbance.
Vibration.

Fractals of the one.

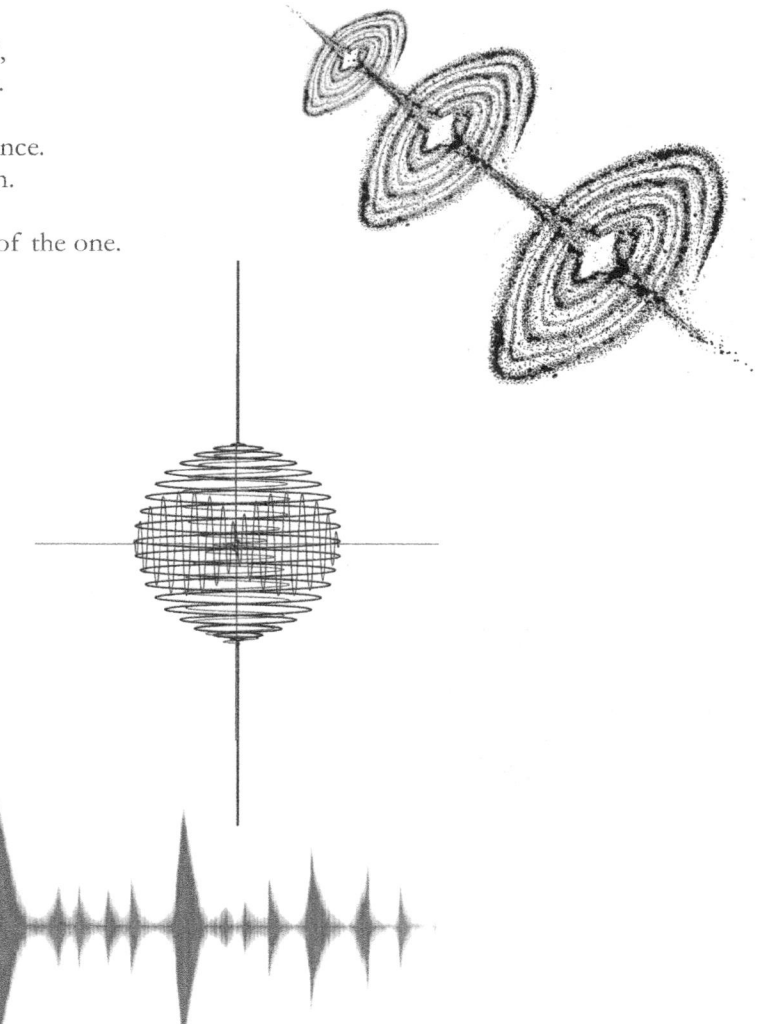

The Bigger Picture/ the smaller picture

Histones

Breather/ one with the universe
Breather,

Open your lungs,
and the cosmos
comes flooding in.

You are the air;

The ether.

The living man.

The all.

Earth,
digesting,
eating,
drinking itself,

passing through its own body.

Consuming
the dust of my rotting,

Bathing
in my waters.

Becoming,
re becoming;

One with the universe.

Burning Man/ entangled with the fabric
All I am,

A rusting man.

Caught,
twisted,
entangled with the fabric.

Pumping,
pulsing,
beating,
drying.

Burning away my flame.

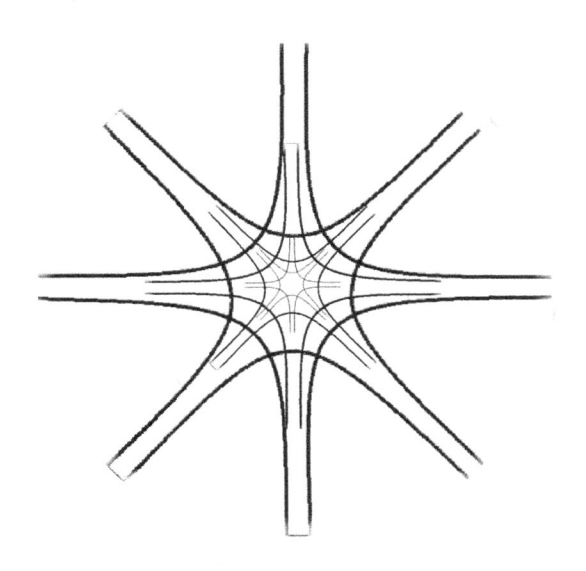

The Roaring Infinite
Look to the stars for answers.

They teach us everything.

Look high
beyond the heavens.

Your destiny;

Only dust,
burning and returning
to the great crystal kingdom.

The heavenly garden.

Dilation/ perception of the image
Dilation is my heart,
eye, and lungs.

Breath.

The universe in my image.

Chapter 5: Inventor

One Who Wonders/ wonders of the world
One who wonders
of the magic of magnets,

expansion, and infinity of a seed,

and all that around him,
in its geometry.

One who takes interests
in coal and soil.

Wowed by volcanic force

and value of its diamond.

One who wonders
of the levitating star.

Wind and its swiftness.

Of colours;

Rain
and its bow.

One who wonders,
wonders of the world
will know.

Natures Favourite Place
Chemistry trickles down
from all the universe
and into you.

Natures favourite place.

The sweet spot.

All connected to the brain;

Collecting information.

Soaking in,
sending vibrations.

Fine tuned,
to sounds, to touch,

sight and smell to
experience itself.

Lighting up the brain.

Alive,

imprinted nerves of the atom

Conquer Space/ the galactic agreement
Tune into the channel.

A galactic agreement.

Join the galaxies

Mind.

Waiting to be conquered.

Concept of Infinity/ god is a concept
In all directions.

Infinite in layers.

Distance, connection, material.

Infinite rebirths.

Infinitely awakening.

Infinite potential
and power.

Take from the Universe
Take from the universe,
knowledge of the substance.

To be tested, observed,
and known.

Study nature,
closely.

It's strikes and whirls.

The abundance of the world.

Mills/ energy flows
Undertow,
magnets and falls.

Motion of the ocean
and earths poles.

Where ever substance flows.

Where ever winds blow.

Heat of the sun.

Wherever nature runs.

Where ever pressure.

Waves
and rivers.

Salt and erosion.

Snow and lightening

Efficient Machine
The universe itself,
perpetual.

You are existence.

Processor and memory.

The greatest aspect of technology.

A closed circuit

A pumping thing.

An infinite seed.

Put together flawlessly.

Fundamental Technology/ fractal technology
I am
but a spark in the wire.

Riding waves,
radiating from the engine.

Heat of its battery;

Swirling through its magnets and rotary.

Merely metal of the device.

The infinite machine.

I am the program,
a technical god.

1s and 0s in the screen.

A motherboard.

Trapped
in its own technology.

Universal Function
A power source.

A battery,

conductor,

amplifier,

transmitter,

receiver.

Storage.

Resistance.

In Times of Your Invention/ in times of your awakening
Inventor,

product of the universe,

Intend forwardness and peace
in times of the epiphany.

Teach man to see.

Your awakening and discoveries.

Replicate
Nature will guide you
with the mark of the universe.

Atom shall replicate;

Geometry.

Course of inventions/ proof of higher intelligence
Tools of stone
so fire, metals
and magnets.

Technology on a course.

Knowledge and
efficiency.

Communication,
consciousness,
control.

Transportation
and
peace.

Each time,
in awe.

Unbelievable.

Molded in the fabric;

Proof of higher intelligence.

Metal Universe
Look out,
into the infinity.

Hydrogen storing
stars and planets.

Moons and asteroids.

The universe,
metal.

The all.

In
and outer space.

Playground of Metals/ the alchemist lives
The alchemist lives.

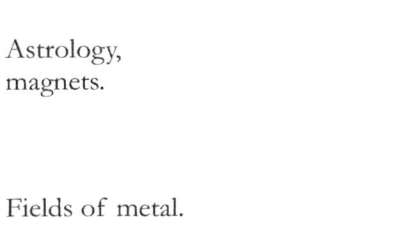

Astrology,
magnets.

Fields of metal.

The electric world.

My sand
and castle.

My playground.

My heaven.

My garden.

Playing with Space/ playing with the density of space
With space, we play.

Take what does not belong
and see it's uses and behavior.

Blooming
in the opposite of its nature.

Iron fusing together like water
in the lesser of space.

Magnets,
draw us a galaxy.

And flowers ends meet.

For one result of an invention
set it in the lesser space.

And the other,
stump it,
in higher resistance.

Coiling
Take magnets,
wrap them in magnets
twist them like a rope
into a coil.

Zap them.

Take it to the earths pole;

Outer space.

Spin it,
rotate it.

Send a current through it.

Put space in space
and reveal the true results of a magnet.

Rings, rings, rings
The universe itself;

Rings around rings.

Belts within belts

In,
around,
as the universe.

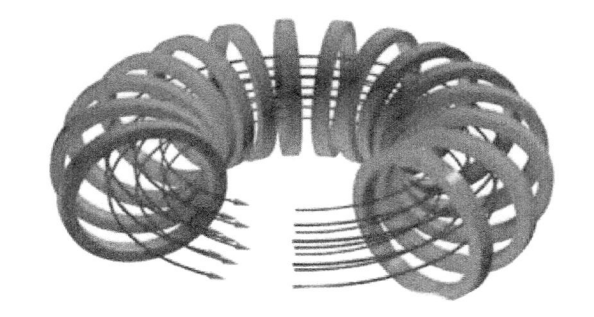

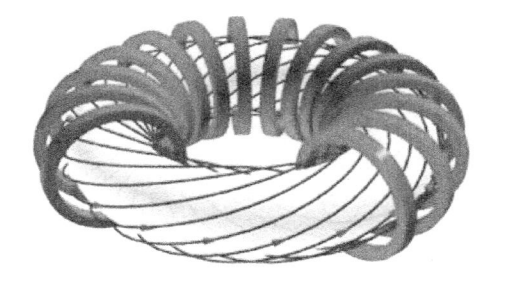

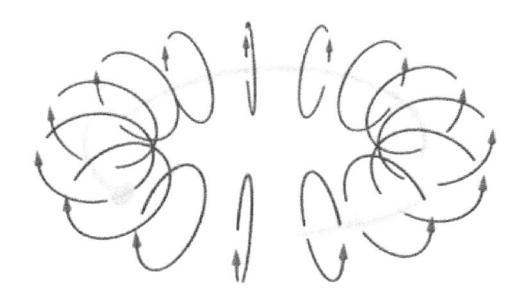

The Atomic Model/ the torus
Men will build
and rebuild the atomic model
until it is correct and functioning exactly.

The arch form of energy.

Taking shape,
the universe.

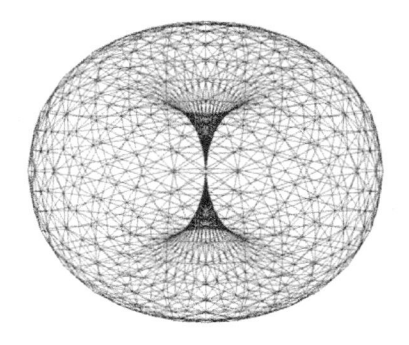

Ancient Technology/ universal technology/ building a magnet
The ancient,

The only;

Universal technology.

Masters of shape and sound,

conscious,
and so discover,

the magnetic field

Transmission
and the harness of power.

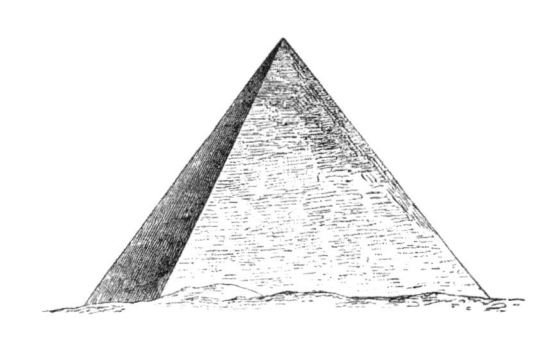

Vacuum/ removing substance
Minimize the air
blocking the specimen.

A magnet to remove the substance.

See further in the fabric

Connect,
or collect the universe.

Magnets, Lenses and Lasers
The future and past,
forever to be discovered.

This universal mechanic lives on forever.

All creatures face these inventions.

Sculpted a society of magnets,
lenses and lasers.

Concentrated heat.

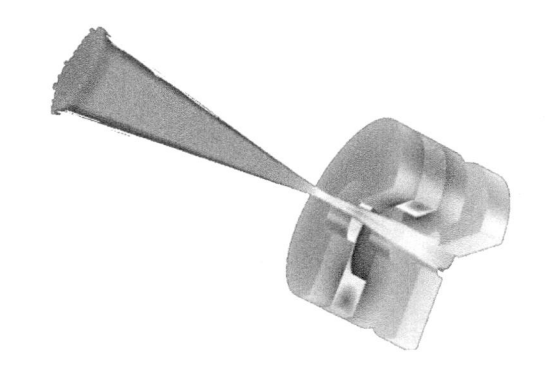

Reality;

Only magnets in a magnet,
laser in a laser
lens in a lens.

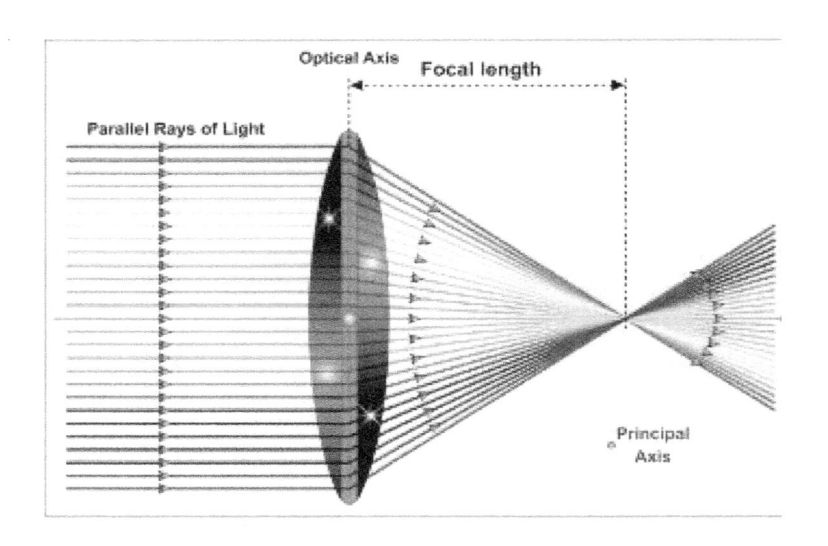

Stretching the Fabric of Reality/ vacuum tech/ the erasure of space
Try to break;

Try to destroy the fabric.

Try to rip space
and discover the source of energy.

Take all air
out of a room.

Shatter
glass out of the windows.

Their shards fall inward.

Collide in the center.

Enter a Magnet/ secret in the stars
Enter a magnet.

Look,
inside the sun.

Find the all;

The infinite.

The creation of space.

Music and colour;

Mimicking the cosmic invention.

The universe;

Vibration.

Listen
to its fractal sound.

Amplified;

Repeating eternally,
ever so faintly,

secrets in the stars.

Space Age/ age of the ether
You shall race,
gather metals in orbit of outer space

Travel,
star to star.

Touch the firmament.

The new age.

Zip Through the System/ magnetic propulsion
Planets
and dust are fuel.

Zig through the field.

Zag,
in an on and off magnet.

Zig
through, around the central solar system.

Zag,
from mercury to neptune.

Zig,
from sun to sun.

Life Around Every Star
There is earth
around every sun.

In every rainbow
and space between.

Where ever blue and green.

Life,
every bubble of the galaxy.

Every speck,
every piece.

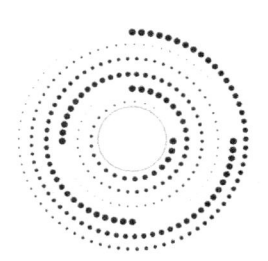

Deep Space Communication/ Galactic Web
There is no distance too far for communication.

Tap into foreign information.

Tune in to universal vibration.

Connect with every species.

Join the intergalactic entities

Expand the web
to the edge of every galaxy.

Aerocraft
Mimic perfect
geometric precession.

Latitude, longitude.

Star and ring.

Opposition of rotation.

Primitive Planet/ enlightened planet
The species have been building forever.

Some shall fight you.

Call you god.

Your craft and knowledge,
magic.

Violent.

And some will laugh at your primitive understanding.

Beings enlightened.

Endless Inventions/ rediscoveries
Hydrogen Fuel
Induction fuel
Diamond battery/salt/ permeability/ earth battery
Magnetic transportation
Magnetic aerocraft/ field propulsion/ gravity fuel
Atmospheric travel/ spin travel
Super coil induction
Induction Rod/ the harness of lightening
Water induction
Wireless energy transmission
Frequency vibration technology
Sound frequency battery
Disease shatter/ frequency resonance tech
Super amplifier/ intergalactic communication/ galaxy net
Universal satellite/ universal antenna/ universal records
Magnetic lens/ vacuum microscope
Output over input
Magnetic beam lock/ levitation tech
Magnetic water purifier
Cold light
Cold weld/ induction weld
Spiral storage/ super compression
Hexagonal structure
Repulsion gear
Body preservation
Electric/ magnetic garden

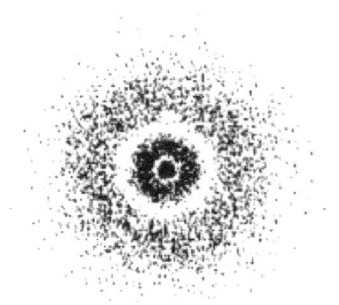

Chapter 6: Conscious/ memory

Ripping Apart the Star/ condense, stretching infinity
I spend time in the stars.

Stretching them apart.

Watching them boil down to the fundamental.

Crushing,
condensing its metal.

I spend time swimming
in drops of dew.

Up and down a flowers tube.

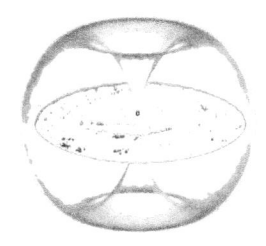

Playing
with the fabric;

Static and planets.

Ripping,
sorting through.

Inside a Magnet/ the inner and outer sides of the system

I am looking at the inside
and outside of a magnet.

Opposite in temperature.

Opposites in motion.

Fractal,
stars.

Galaxies as one
potential center.

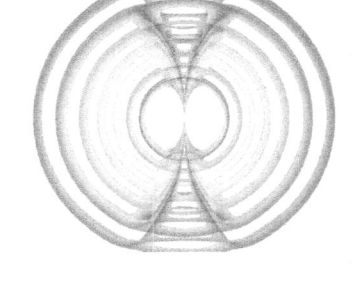

An engine.

A system,
self generating.

The inner,
and outer side of the universe.

The Toroidal Fabric
All is magnetic;
all is falling.

All is electric.
All is burning.

The universe,

Toroidal fields of fabric.

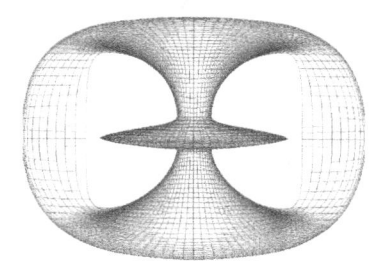

The X, and Y/ the 'object'/ function of existence/ nullspace/ lesser space/ vacuum/ cause of motion/ spin/ point source/ the universal engine
Pole/ Equator

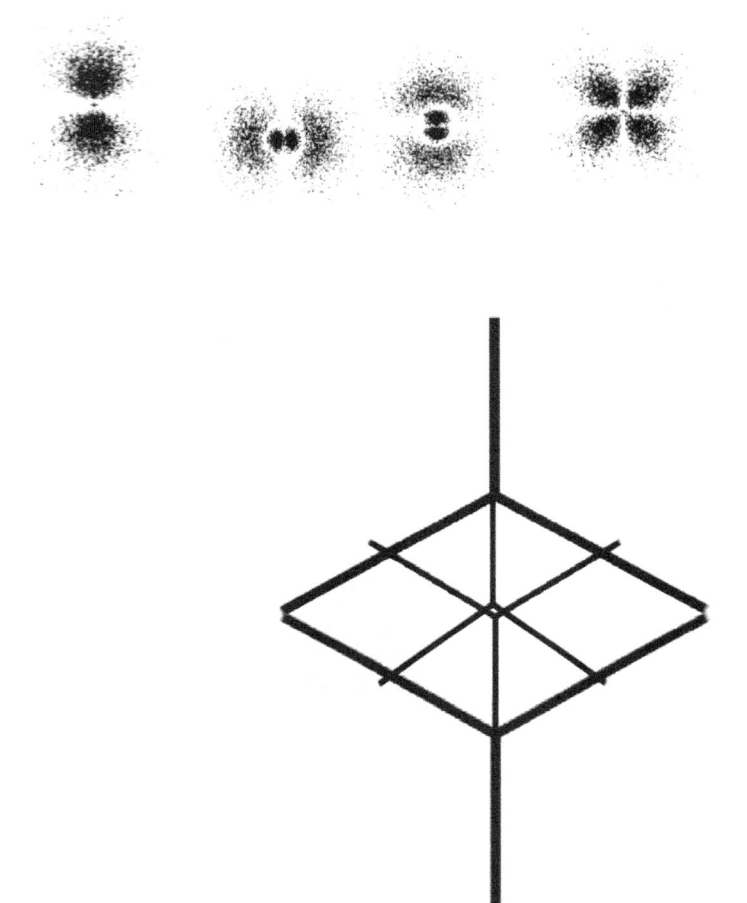

Magnet/ mass

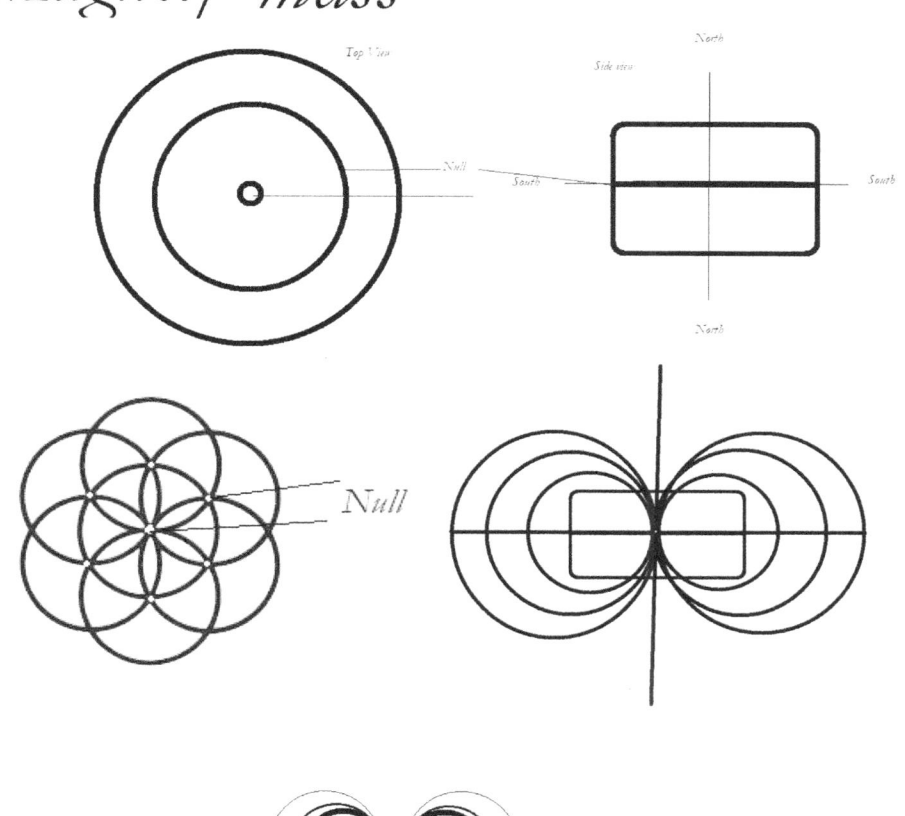

The Pull and Throw/ breath of the star/ in, out/ motion
Absorbing,
radiating,

pulling,
throwing the atom.

In, out.

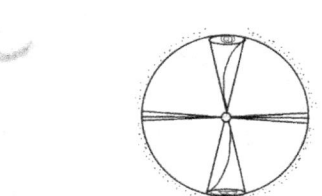

Pulsing,
breath of a star.

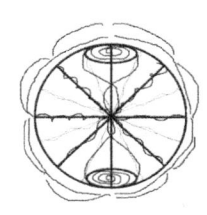

Centripetal.
Centrifugal.

Fluctuating metals.

The universe making magnets,
entrapping its opposite.

Unwinding its source.

Vortex of Galaxies
Man stands,
in the violent,
thrashing,
roaring vortex.

Tornadoes of galaxies
inside galaxies.

So compressed,
experiencing the illusion of stillness.

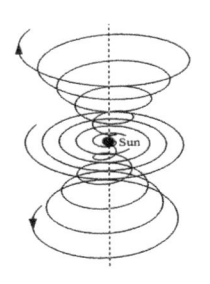

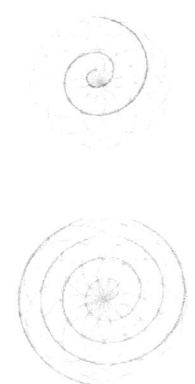

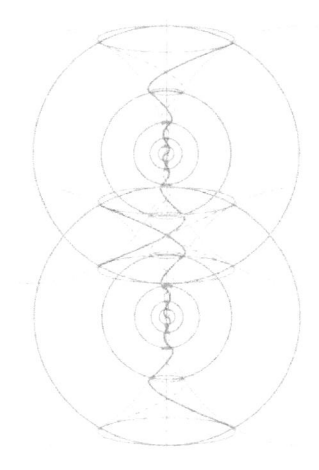

Fractal Existence/ symmetrical/ the oscillating drop
Lines of potential/ electric magnetic lines/ null space

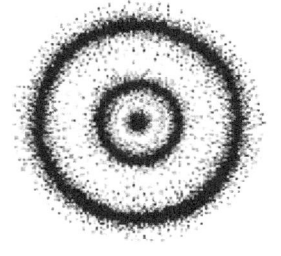

Rainbow Star
A warm pocket in the outer cool ocean.

A collision of space.

A rainbow.

Planets.

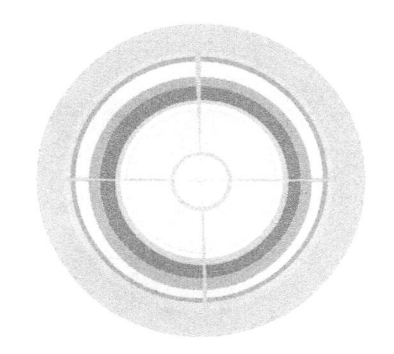

The colourful layers of hydrogen.

Layers of the Universe/ octaves

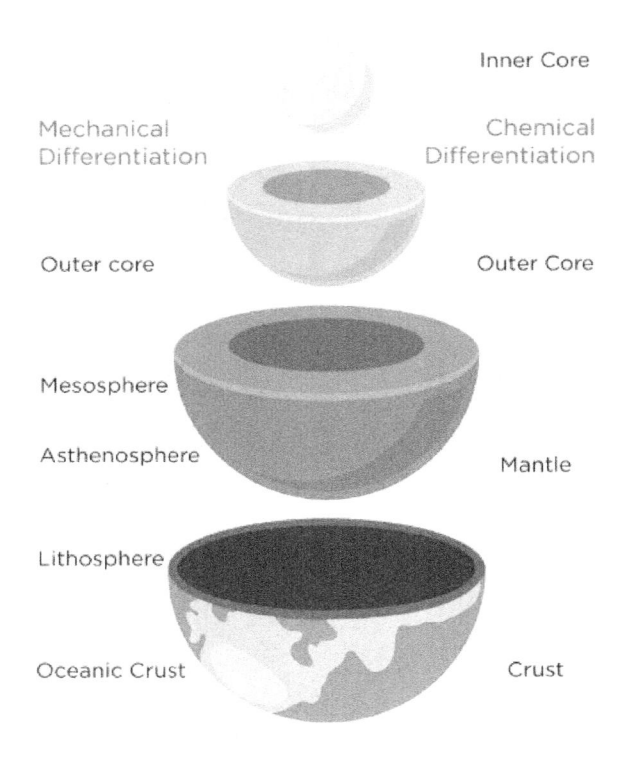

Inner Core

Mechanical Differentiation

Chemical Differentiation

Outer core

Outer Core

Mesosphere

Asthenosphere

Mantle

Lithosphere

Oceanic Crust

Crust

The Star Beyond Ours/the inner, outer system/ the spinning magnet/ belt of stars

Beyond the stars.

Octaves beyond this;

Rings of space,
fields of toruses
surround us.

outer stars
center star

Star inside stars.

Firmament.

Moving belts,
on the machine that is acceleration.

Potential procession.

Magnetic gears.

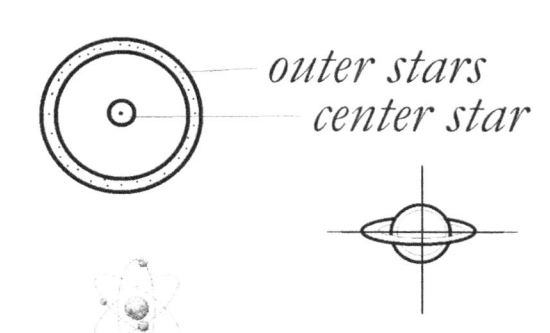

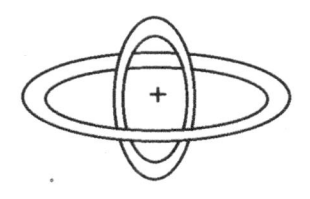

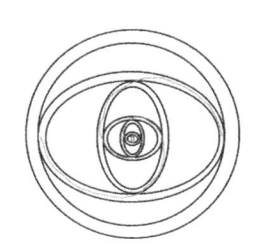

Ice and Diamond/ hexagonal/ cubic
The closest, and furthest structure possible.

The compression,
the capacitance,
the expansion of the fundamental.

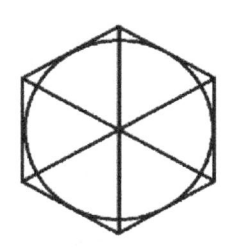

Expansion of the Field

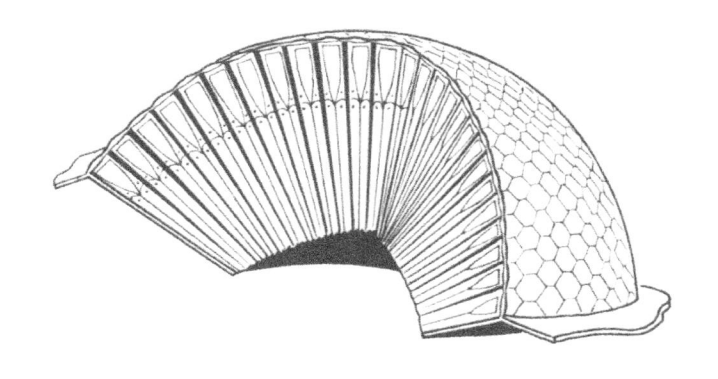

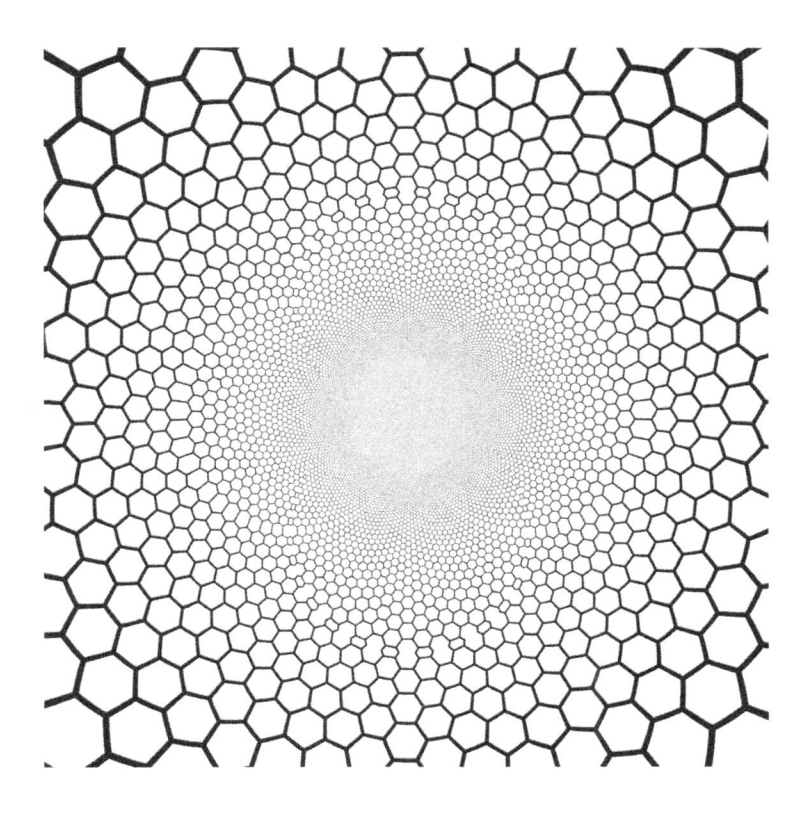

Shadow
Overcasted is the shadow
over the core.

Planets beyond the stars.

Crust of earth,
towering over the distant sparks.

Shining in the cool place of the system.

The Crystal Firmament/ crystal cave/ geode/ the hollow sturdy stone/ grain of sand/ the outer dome
A geode,
a crystal cave.

Sand.

Solar system.

The outer dome.

The greater hollow sturdy stone.

The burning firmament wall.

Patina
Pulled to surface.

Oxidation.

Trading places,

a disturbance.

The lesser seeping in
expanding the substance.

Geometry of the
universe pushing though.

Rust.
Patina.

Salt,
crystal.

Memory/ angle, sound, colour/ information
Memory goes on.

Angle,
sound,
colour.

The burning,
the falling.

Discharge,

in the shape of the universe.

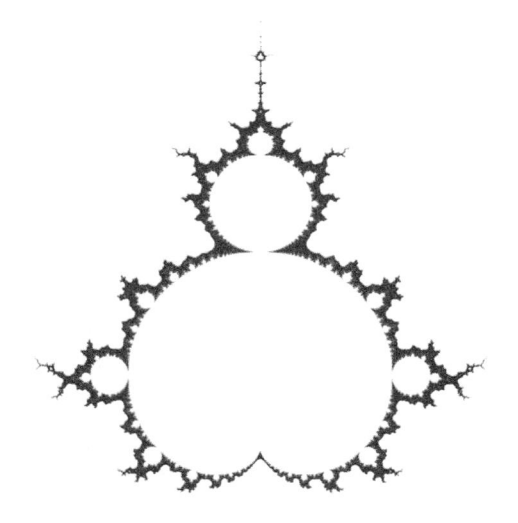

GOD/ the free falling universe/ the dance of heat
Falling, falling
is the universe.

On, and on,
an eternity through the fabric.

Accelerating
in the shape of god
through the galaxies.

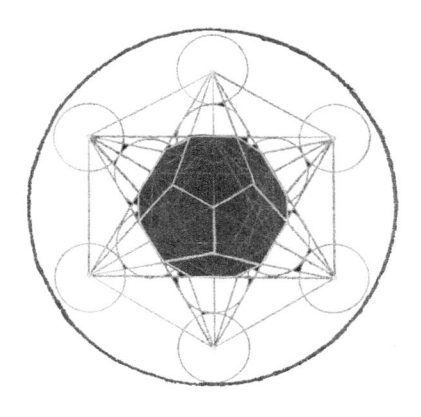

Geometry of the Infinite/ geometry of the vein

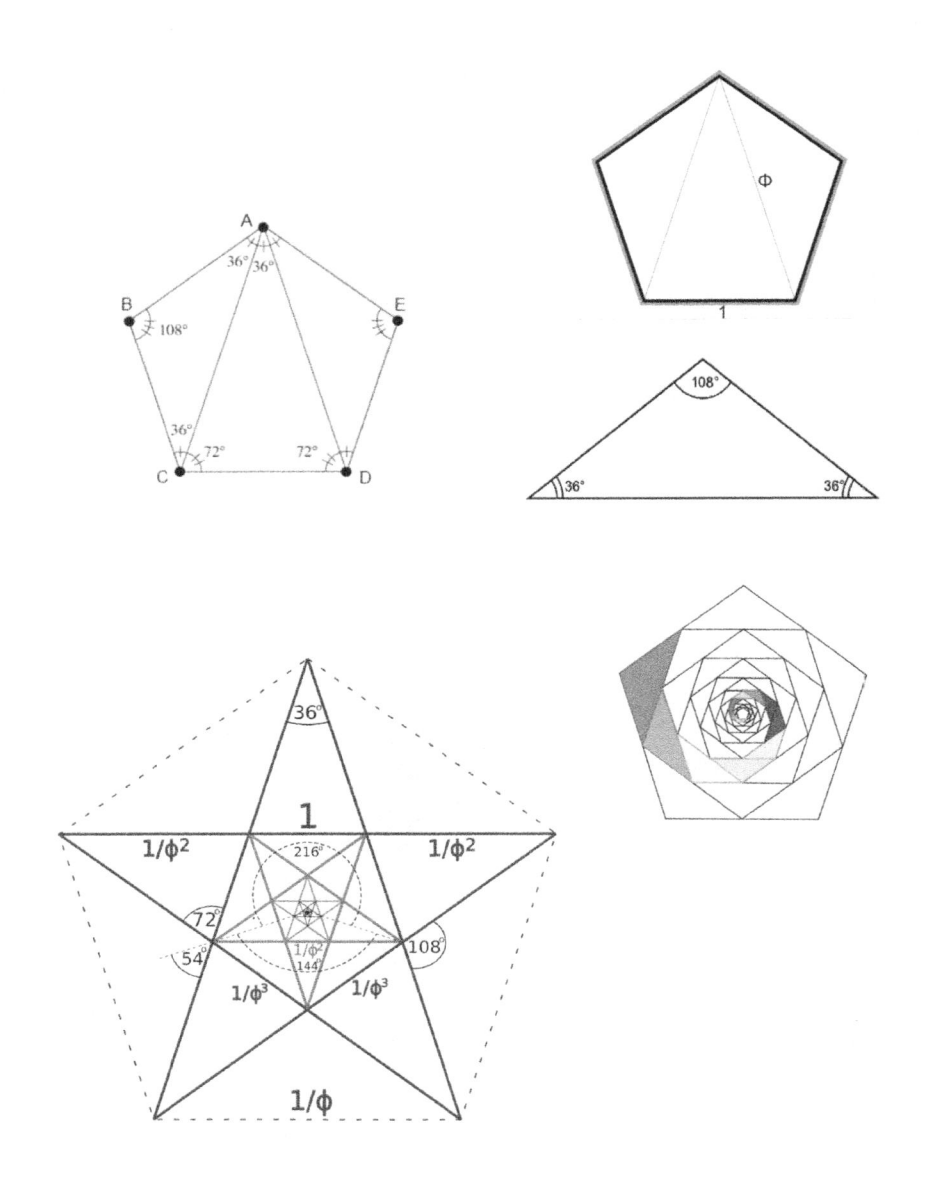

Spiral Universe
Carbon, corrosion
compacted cosmos,
coming out from the crust.

Coiled
infinite fractal pattern.

All the pretty colours.

Burned,
but not gone.

Twisted into seeds.

Unraveled veins
into branch, stem, pedal and leaves.

The tree.

A spiral.

Seed/ plant

induction
capacitance
radiation / discharge

The Unfurling Infinity/ the infinitely compressed universe

Man exists in
and as the heavenly garden.

Living the unfolding galaxies.

Peeling back
the unfurling infinity.

Breathing in its juices.

Walking upon its rind.

The plant,
the flower,
the tree.

The vegetable,
the fruit.

The seed.

The All; The Universe/ the universe is
The universe is;

A crystal,
a solar system,
and diamond.

The all inside all.

A rainbow,
a focal point,

The fabric.

The living creature.

Star and Cell
Stars, cells;

Magnetic.

The galaxy.

The body.

Earth; The Universe
Find god;

A great vein.

A fractal vibration of the spinning.

Earth,
atom;

The universe.

Infinity.

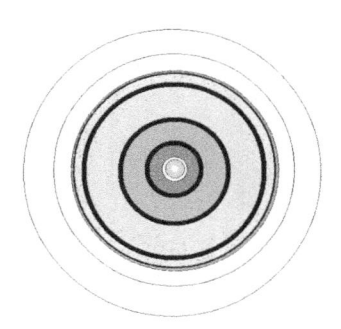

Earth/ atom

Spirals in the Sand/calm water/ sea stars
Laying upon the surface,
spirals in the sand.

Product of the all.

Calm waters
washing in seas stars,
shell and coral.

Chapter 7: Insanity/ philosophy

Incomplete/ unworthy poetry
There are a few missing concepts
in the dictionary.

Every single thing is a contradiction.

Mostly nonsense.

And one thousand pages too long.

Incomplete.

Irrelevant.

It is like you have not finished the sentence.

I cannot understand what you are saying.

Missing wide gaps of data.

The unity of existence;

Missing root of knowledge.

Every word,
every assumption;

Unworthy poetry.

False Information/ theory
Crammed into your head,
false information.

False conclusions.

As science still exists,
the theory still exists.

Searching for the biggest answer.

Obviously
we have not peaked.

With many questions still to be asked.

Still studying,
still experimenting.

Knowing nothing.

Still to be humbled.

Debate
Still debating;

God.

Science.

Reality.

What is.

How it works.

Failing to take the information
back to the beginning.

Misjudging the fundamental.

Not yet conscious of the substance.

Dancing Around the Root Cause/ turtles all the way down
Stacking imaginary objects.

It is turtles all the way down.

One props up the other.

Dancing so lightly around the root cause.

Shoved under the carpet.

The silly explanation.

Parrot/ Mimic/ the great impressionist
I have spent so much time
mocking you.

I am a mimic.

A parrot.

The copy cat.

A great impressionist.

Caveman and the Stone Ax/ modern caveman
The caveman built a stone ax and cut down
one thousand trees.

And still,
no idea of the universal mechanic.

His priority;

To only build
and to eat.

Starting from Scratch/ shoulders of giants
I am starting from scratch,
standing on the shoulders of giants.

Illusion of the Word/ objectified/ the word does not exist
Language and meaningless sounds.

They hold no value.

Objectified and untrue.

Not fundamental.

He who does not speak in poetic tongue
be pummeled.

You have stepped over the boundaries.

Outside of truth.

Beyond the criteria.

Into imagination.

Correction/ instant change
It is not too late
to correct all that has been done
and set things straight.

To shift our perspective and thought process.

Its not too late to see everything as one.

To live the right way.

We could change in an instant.

Conceptual/ becoming conscious of the fundamental
The universe consists of very little.

And all that exists
is consciousness.

Aware of its universal function.

Illusion of Existence/ the illusion of creation
Imagine the substance,
already there.

The echo of existence.

A fractal of the happening.

Creation and destruction,
an illusion.

Illusion of the Phenomena
Light
separation
chaos

creation
destruction
emptiness

time
weight
direction

size
self
death

the object
freedom
silence
darkness

Frequencies of the Universe/ octave
Sound
colour
static
snow
trees
flower

fire, water, earth, air.
All that is space.
And all that is the universe.

mountains
volcano
lightening
electricity
lava
planet, moon, star, meteor
solar system
firmament
dna

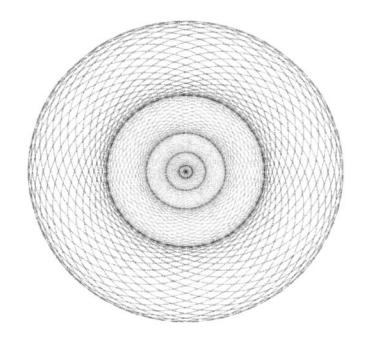

Octaves,
frequency of heat.

Illusion of Size/ "particle and star"/ "the string and hole"/
Size is the illusion.

Do not be fooled by law.

No difference between a physicist, and astronomer.

No difference between the particle and star.

String and black hole.

The Illusion of Density / the illusion of perception
This air.

It is so fascinating.

Out there.

In here.

Packed, and spread.

The illusion of density.

So big, so little
and out of perspective.

Illusion of the State/ "ice, solid, gas"/ the illusion of density/ the illusion of mass
No solid.
No liquid.
No gas.

More or less.

The illusion of mass
searching for balance and rest.

Indestructible Concept of Existence
No water could drown,
no heat could burn,
no stone could crush;

No vacuum too powerful.

I am indestructible.

There is no space thin enough to break.

The universe could never shatter,
never die.

Never be ruined, tarnished or destroyed.

Silence Does Not Exist/ the sound of breathing.
The almighty in motion.

No stillness,
no silence.

The universe, breathing.

The Object Does Not Exist
The object does not exist.

Only frequency of heat and motion.

A happening.

A verb.

A presence,

Law.

Not a thing.

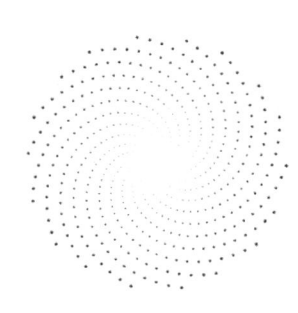

The Illusion of "Dimension"
The all.

Existence.

The inside and out,
the potential,
the infinity.

The one;

Reality.

The Illusion of Inertia
All you see,
is only temporary.

A collision.

A sound.

A magnet,

a motion.

Illusion of Sound/ disturbance/ Illusion of the sphere/ song of the spheres/ illusion of music
All at which he laughs,
and all he cries.

And all he breathes,

Sound of the universe.

Speaking his existence.

The illusion of the spheres.

Disturbance.

Clashing in the swirling ether.

"Nothing" Does Not Exist/ Something rather than nothing/ the illusion of creation/ the illusion of emptiness/ the lesser space/ the magnetic field
It is the standing definition of itself.

Existence.

That which is.

The illusion of creation.

The something rather than nothing.

The Illusion of Zero/ the lesser space
The infinity.

The vacuum.

The lesser space.

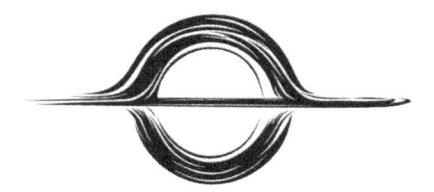

Illusion of Infinity/ the illusion of space/ illusion of the ether/ The illusion of potential
Every single thing you have named,
experience the illusion.

Caught in awe of its potential.

The illusion of space.

The infinity.

The ether.

The inner, the outer, the all.

In the infinite potential that is existence.

The Number Does Not Exist/ the insanity of measuring potential
One would go insane
trying to measure the uncountable.

Numbers do not exist

One,
and infinity.

The more,
the less

Equal and resonant.

Concept of the all.

Pure potential.

Patterns of Nature/ fascinated with the fabric/ the fractal universal one
The same pattern in the tree
exists in your eyes, and galaxy.

I can plainly see the magic of the world and all the stars
twisted up.

Staring hard into the fabric.

The fractal universal one.

Everywhere.

Fascinated by its present hiding.

The Planets Sing
Planets press together,
tightening the fabric,
and together,
the solar system,
a symphony.

Point Source/ the fundamental
We are but the tip of something bigger.

The peak of a fading spark.

The end of the flame.

Point of a leaf

Static left in the air.

An electromagnet.

Part of the song.

The center,
and the edge of our stars.

The Illusion of the Universe/ illusion of acceleration

Space is the
mechanic of that which exists.

All aspects of nature,

coils in motion.

All magnetic,
all electric,

Acceleration.

And space is all there is.

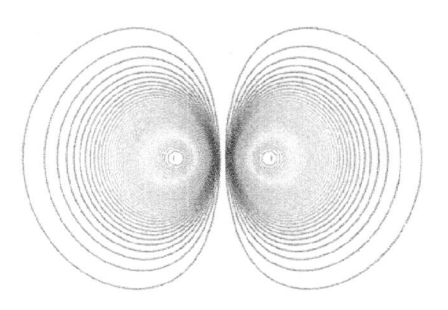

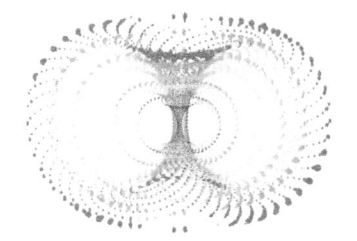

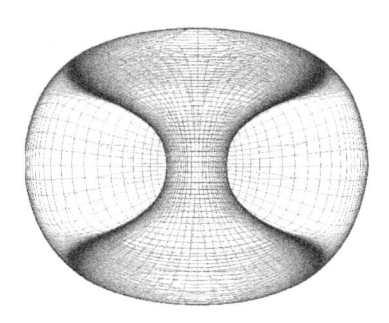

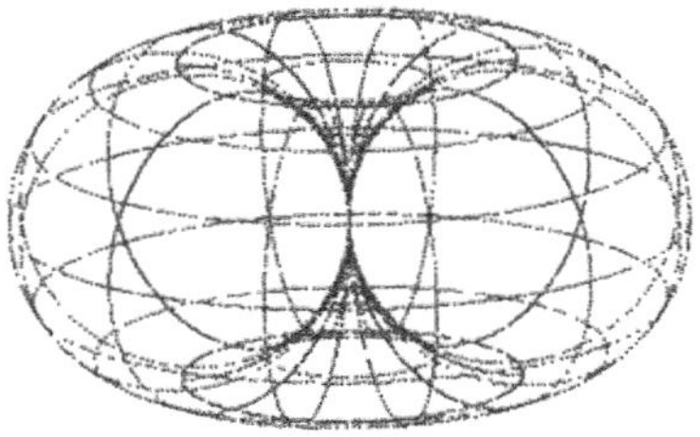

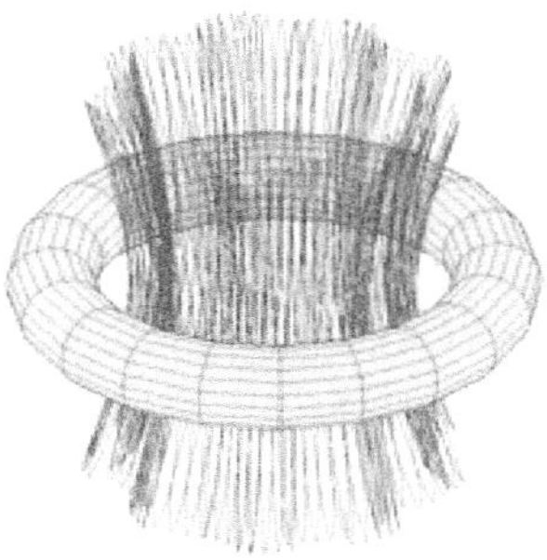

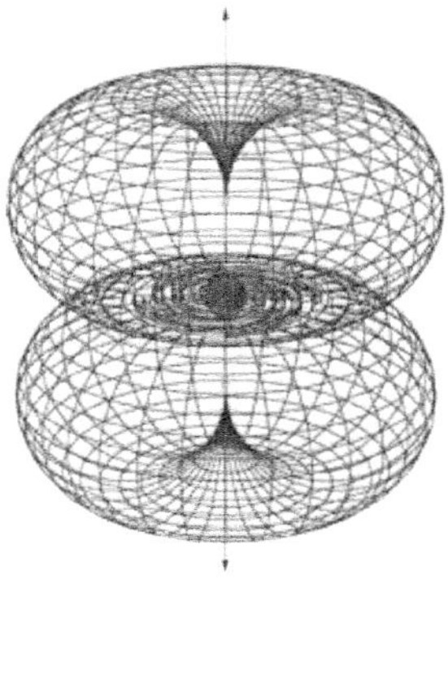

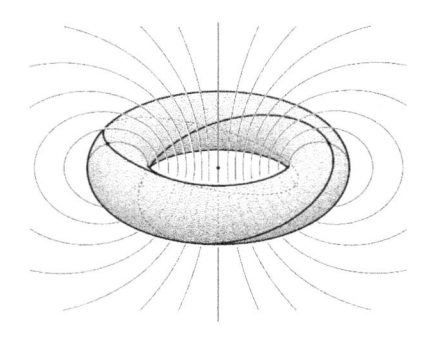

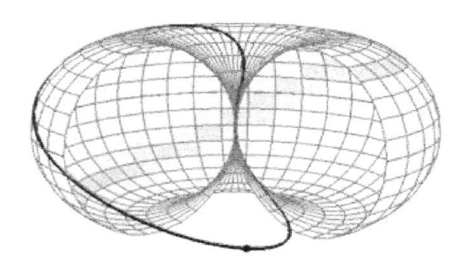

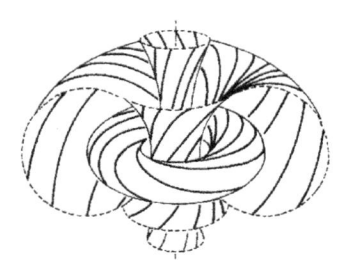

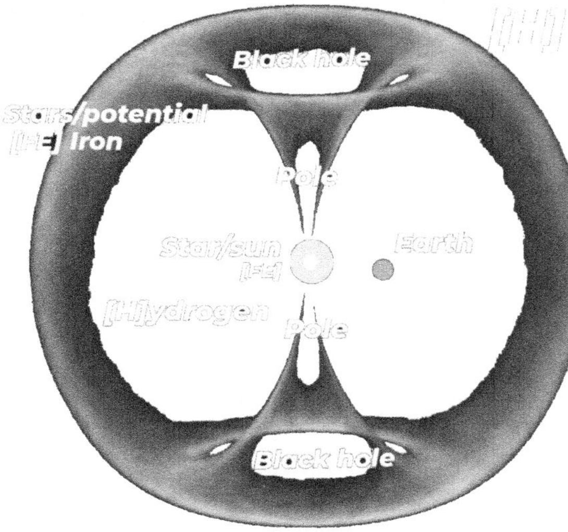
Black hole
Stars/potential
[FE] Iron
Pole
Star/sun
Earth
[H]ydrogen
Pole
Black hole

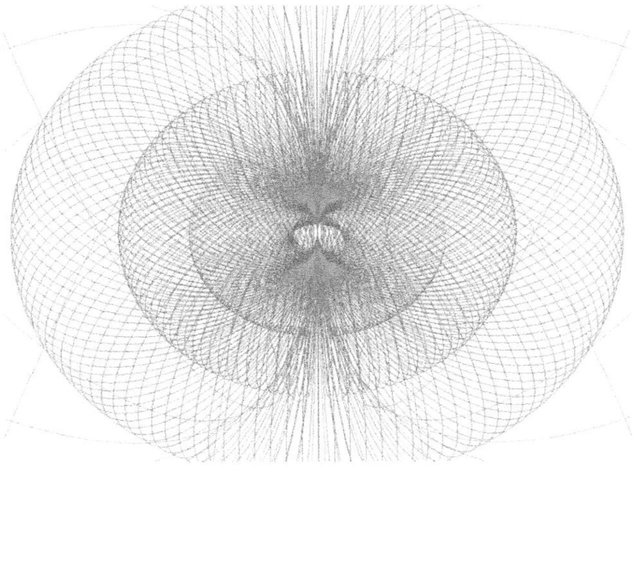

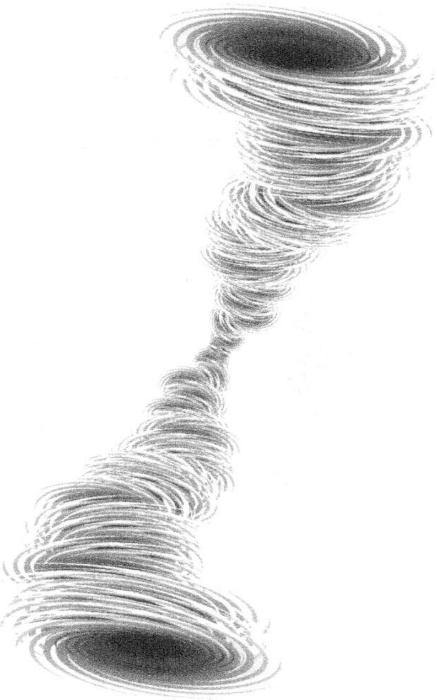

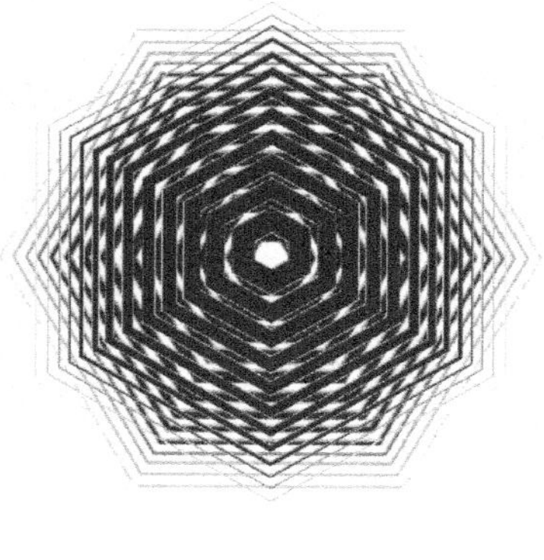

The Vacuum/ geometry of the sphere/ acceleration/ the "magnet"
A vacuum center.

The lesser space;
the magnet.

Stars held up
by the clashing atom,

a spiral induction.

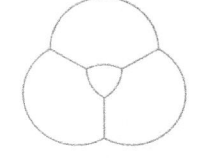

Tangling,
twisting the fabric.

Inhaled,

Regurgitating
its packed potential.

Magnetism.

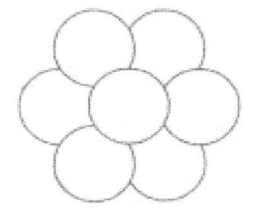

The lesser space of the universe.

The singularity.

The sun,
mass,

welded metal.

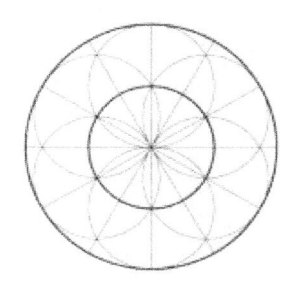

Induction, Capacitance, Discharge, Resonance/ the collapse function/ direction does not exist
Outward radiation.

Inward magnetism.

Centripetal, centrifugal.

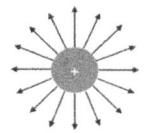

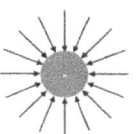

Pulse of the stars

The clashing primordial disturbing the field.

The collapsing function.

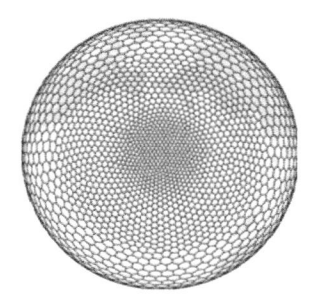

Birth of the Meteor / creation of the magnet
Stars become the planet,
and planets become the star.

Crushing,
compacted in the universal hydrogen.

And out from the light,

birthed a meteor.

Caught in the layer of water to rust.

Straying toward
and away from the heavens.

Freezing,
Igniting

Outside of the boundaries of the layer.

The Iron All/ rust in the wind
No more than a dot in the sky.

A speck in the sand.

Rust is in the wind.

A grain of salt in the ocean.

Caught in the toroidal substance.

Corroding
We,
the universe
are only bits of the great hydrogen;

The metal.

Washing in and out of the ocean.

Ground down
by the waves.

The Tilling of Rain
Water tills up the metal,

rust.

Rain
tilling the garden.

Digging into the iron.

Fluffed,
Bringing out its potential.

Sand, Dirt and Soil/ what man calls death/ mud/mud, and dirt/ oil
I am life.

What man calls death.

Sand,
dirt
and soil.

Mud, moisture, the oils.

Ash,
soot
and coal.

Extract of the universe.

The Source of Life
Inside the iron all,
every single thing.

Packed potential.

thrown into the layer of balance.

Water and air.

The perfect throw.

The source of life.

Shifting Through the Galaxy/ illusion of the plant/ loaded spring/ illusion of the galaxy/ the coiling, twisted fabric
The coiling fabric.

Illusion of the plant,
the atom and galaxy.

Unfolding spiral motion.

Shifting through the medium.

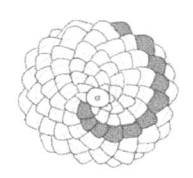

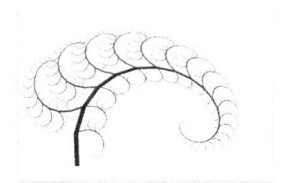

Rind/ visual of the field
The rind on all the fruit,

Their skin, and innards
the screen,

the field.

Secrets of the metals.

Secrets of the sun.

Shapes of frequency,

Map of the galaxy.

The Screen of Reality
Hexagonal screen pattern.

The fabric before you.

The oscillating magnetic, electric field.

The web.

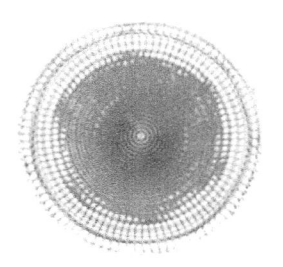

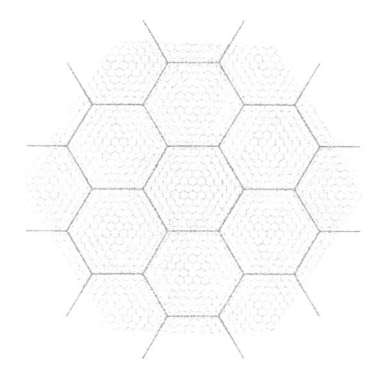

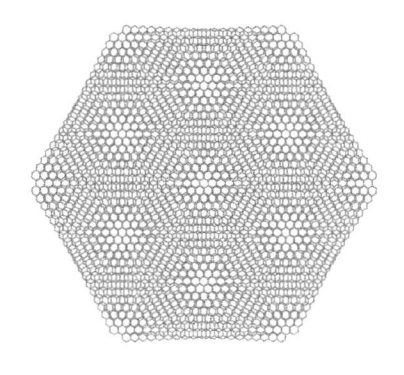

Stretched or Crushed/ the burning web
The body will burn,
or freeze,
where ever it is placed.

Ripped
in the cool, and hot spots of space.

Crushed
burned,

into oscillation of rings.

Sacred geometry.

Compression,
expansion
into cubes.

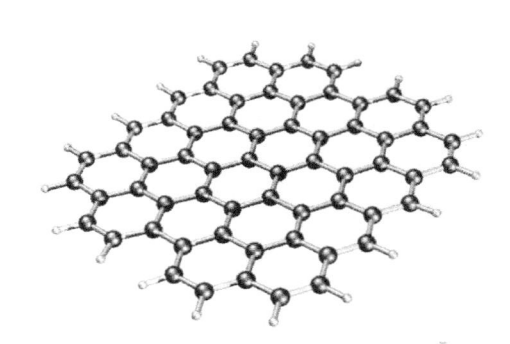

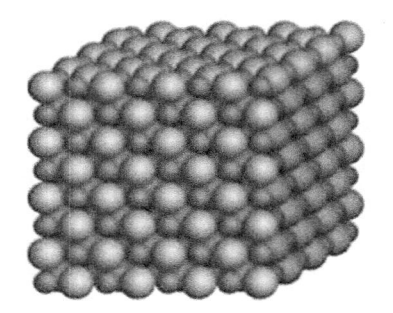

Freezing/ capped column/fruits of the phenomenon

The X and Y of Motion
The sun soaking earths water,

letting it loose in its shadow.

Fog, air, the cloud.
the wind, rain and waves.

Weather.

The x and y motions.

The Inverse of the Universe
I stand over all the gorgeous, bright galaxies.

Like a giant,
stomping on all the pretty colours.

Parent of motion.

I wear the universe;

My outer skin.

The X and Y of existence.

The inverse of the universe.

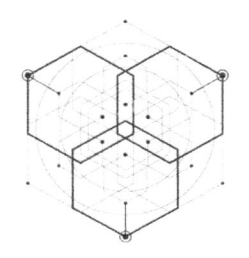

The original sin.

Philosophy/ phi
The divine proportion

Unification.

The one, the all.

The art of motion.

Law that governs the universe.

Shapes of the fabric.

The root of reality.

The knowledge of everything.

Geometry of man;

God,
and thy love for wisdom.

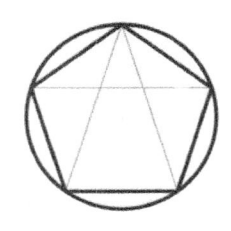

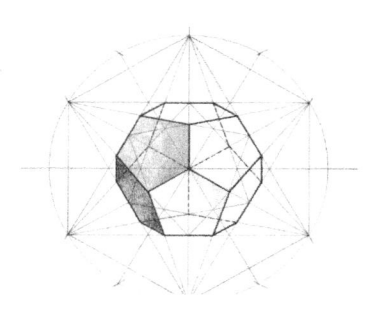

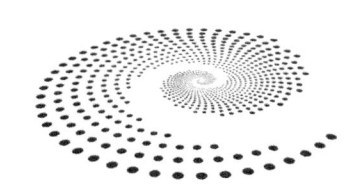

Truth of the Matter/ poetry and magnetism

I will leave you with the dark,
enlightening truth.

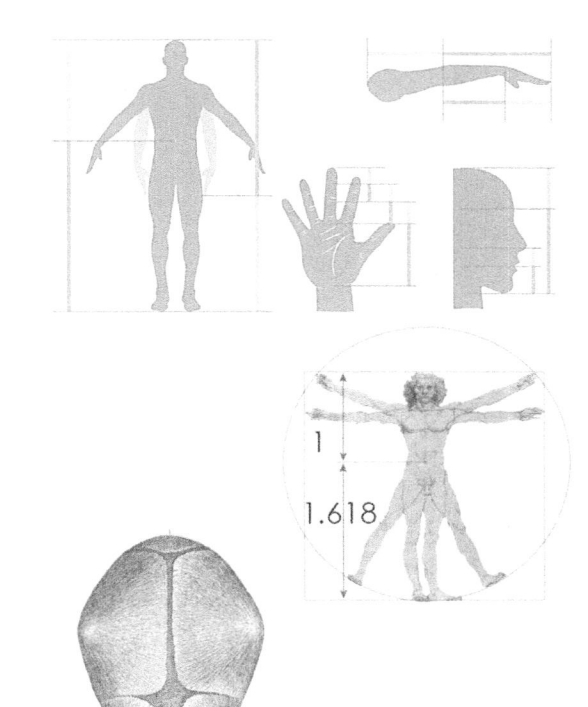

It is you.

The one.

God of the earth.

It,
motion,
and that,
mind.

Poetry,
magnetism.

That which is;

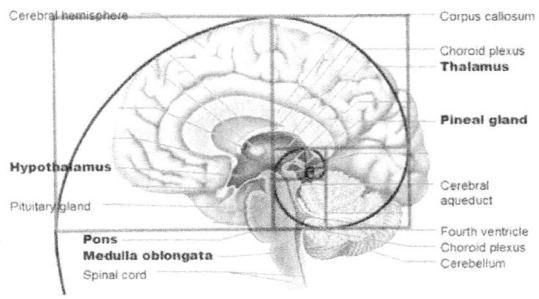

Laughter.

The breath,
and joke of consciousness.

ENERGY
All
ATOM-UNIVERSE/MIND/EXISTENCE
ILLUSION
Radiation
Magnetism
Heat/motion
Vibration
SPACE
Black Hole
MATTER
Repulsion
Acceleration
Evaporation
Rain
(Water)
Potential
Hydrogen
Metal
Torus Field
Space (Air)
Atmos
Water
Life
Mantle
Core
(Fire)
(Earth)
137.5077
You Are Here
Electric
Dielectric
STARS LIFE
Empty Space
Light
Separation
Chaos
Weight
Time
Death
Direction
Size
State of Matter
Induction
Capacitance
Discharge
Resistance

Made in the USA
Monee, IL
09 January 2025